THE QUOTABLE
Amelia Earhart

THE QUOTABLE *Amelia Earhart*

EDITED BY Michele Wehrwein Albion

UNIVERSITY OF NEW MEXICO PRESS | ALBUQUERQUE

© 2015 by the University of New Mexico Press
All rights reserved. Published 2015
Printed in the United States of America
20 19 18 17 16 15   1 2 3 4 5 6

Library of Congress Cataloging-in-Publication Data
Earhart, Amelia, 1897–1937.
[Quotations. Selections]
The quotable Amelia Earhart /
edited by Michele Wehrwein Albion. — First [edition].
pages cm
Includes bibliographical references and index.
ISBN 978-0-8263-4562-2 (cloth : alk. paper) —
ISBN 978-0-8263-4563-9 (electronic)
1. Earhart, Amelia, 1897–1937—Quotations.
I. Albion, Michele Wehrwein, editor.
II. Title.
TL540.E3A3 2015
081—dc23

2014047528

Cover illustration: Amelia Earhart in Hawaii, courtesy of
the Pacific Aviation Museum
Designed by Felicia Cedillos
Composed in Minion 10.25/13.5
Display fonts are Aspire and Gil Sans Std

*For the wonderful staff of the Dover Public Library in Dover,
New Hampshire, who bring knowledge, joy,
and the spirit of adventure to their patrons every day*

Contents

Preface and Acknowledgments ix

Chronology xiii

1. On Flying Planes and Pilots 1
2. On Earhart's Own Flights 19
3. On the Aviation Industry 41
4. On Machines and Transportation 51
5. On Business and Money 57
6. On Work 65
7. On Politics and Government 75
8. On War 81
9. On Education 89
10. On Gender and Age 97
11. On Marriage, Parenting, and Birth Control 111
12. On Human Qualities and Emotions 123
13. On Health and Exercise 133
14. On Fame and the Press 139
15. Miscellaneous 151

16. Amelia Earhart on Herself   167
17. Amelia Earhart on Others   175
18. Others on Amelia Earhart   183

Notes   205
Bibliography   243
Index   247

Preface and Acknowledgments

It is the most honest motive for the majority of mankind's achievements. To want in one's own heart to do a thing for its own sake; to enjoy doing it; to concentrate all of one's energies upon it—that is not only the surest guarantee of its success, it is also being truly oneself.[*]

—AMELIA EARHART, date unknown

Amelia Earhart was a fearless pioneer, an accomplished record-breaking pilot, and a tireless advocate for women's rights, but what people most remember about her is that she was lost. On July 2, 1937, while on the last leg of an ambitious round-the-world flight, she and her navigator, Fred Noonan, disappeared. They were never heard from again.

In the decades since, people have put forth various theories to solve the mystery. Some allege that she crash-landed on a Pacific island and survived. Others claim that she died or was captured by the Japanese.[†] The most likely explanation, of course, is that she and her navigator ran out of fuel, crashed, and died.

But as historian A. Bowdoin Van Riper explains, the term *disappeared* "glosses over the grim details of their final moments. It

---

[*] Putnam, *Soaring Wings*, 101.
[†] This volume does not seek to further discuss Earhart's disappearance. Readers seeking such an understanding would be advised to read one of the many excellent Earhart biographies or other scholarly sources on the subject.

even suggests, in a way that 'lost at sea' does not, that those lost have departed this life for the next in the most direct way possible—flying until, somewhere beyond the sky, they reach Heaven." In short, we prefer the euphemism, and with it the possibility that her story did not end tragically.

Unfortunately, the beacon focused on Earhart's disappearance has long obscured her daring accomplishments and opinions. The young pilot was a wise, well-spoken adventurer who challenged and inspired individual women and men, her nation, and indeed the world. *The Quotable Amelia Earhart* seeks to provide a concise, documented collection of Earhart's quotations so that her words, as well as her achievements, may inspire a new generation.

Earhart was not a lone aviatrix. There were many other women pilots—Bessie Coleman, Louise Thaden, Ruth Nichols, Amy Johnson, Anne Morrow Lindbergh, and Blanche Noyes, to name a few. But Earhart alone became the female symbol of adventure, fearlessness, and the pioneering spirit of our nation. The fact that she encouraged women to step beyond the narrow confines of their traditional roles seems to have been largely lost. But the generation of women that grew up in Earhart's shadow had no difficulty becoming Rosie the Riveter during World War II, largely because Earhart told them when they were girls that they could do it.

Amelia Earhart was called Lady Lindy because of her resemblance to aviator Charles Lindbergh, who made his solo Atlantic crossing five years before hers. Unlike the taciturn Lindbergh, Earhart was at ease with the public and press. In her first interview, for the *Boston Daily Globe*, she revealed herself to be an eloquent spokesperson, even before her first transatlantic crossing.*

For the next ten years Earhart engaged the nation and the world, in interviews, on the radio, in magazine columns and books she authored, in private letters, and in hundreds of personal appearances. Topics discussed included flying, of course, but also politics, business, money, technology, health, and war, to name a few.

The source material for Earhart's quotes is varied. In addition to newspaper and magazine interviews, she wrote letters to pilots and friends like Eleanor Roosevelt. Her correspondence with her mother, sister, and husband reveals more frank, unvarnished opinions. Because they were meant to remain private, they often employ slang and nontraditional spelling.

Earhart authored three books: *20 Hrs., 40 Min.: Our Flight in the Friendship*; *The Fun of It*; and *Last Flight* (issued posthumously). Each was written and published hastily to capitalize on her popularity following a record-breaking flight. While the writing is uneven, the books show her to be thoughtful and articulate.

The majority of quotations span only a decade, from her first published interview in 1927 to her disappearance in 1937. She died on the cusp of her fortieth birthday. It makes one pause to think what wonders she might have accomplished and what she might have said and done had she lived for another decade.

I am deeply grateful to a number of organizations and individuals who helped make *The Quotable Amelia Earhart* possible. Thank

---

* "Urges Women Take Up Flying," *Boston Daily Globe*, June 26, 1927.

you to the Dover Public Library in Dover, New Hampshire, especially to interlibrary loan librarian S. V. Thanks also to the University of New Hampshire's Dimond Library, with its excellent collection of twentieth-century periodicals, and to the library's staff for their invaluable assistance. I also appreciate the time and expertise of archivist Jonathan Smith at the Chautauqua Archives; Ellen M. Shea at the Schlesinger Library, Radcliffe Institute for Advanced Study, Harvard University; archivist Amanda M. Fulcher at the National Society of the Daughters of the American Revolution; archives coordinator James Hoyle at the British Pathe Archives; and curator Marcus E. Eckhardt from the Herbert Hoover Presidential Library-Museum. Special recognition to proofreader Peg Goldstein, who could see what I could not. Last, thanks to my children—Zoe, Noah, Sarah, and Matthew—for their constant support.

Chronology

July 24, 1897	Amelia Mary Earhart is born in Atchison, Kansas.
1916	Graduates from Hyde Park High School in Chicago.
1917	Works as a Voluntary Aid Detachment nurse in Toronto, Canada, during World War I.
1919	Enrolls as a premed student at Columbia University.
1920	Leaves Columbia University. Moves to California to live with her parents. Takes first airplane flight.
1921	Takes flying lessons with Neta Snook. Buys Kinnear Airster biplane.
1922	Sets unofficial women's flying altitude record of 14,000 feet.
1925–1928	Works as a social worker at Denison House in Boston.
1927	Proposes forming an organization for women pilots.

1928	Becomes the first woman to cross the Atlantic on the *Friendship* with Wilmer Stultz and Louis Gordon. Buys Avro Avian plane from Lady Mary Heath. Writes *20 Hrs. 40 Min.: Our Flight in the Friendship*.
1929	Buys single-engine Lockheed Vega airplane. Places third in the Women's Air Derby. Helps found the Ninety-Nines, an organization of female pilots. Works for Transcontinental Air Transport.
1930	Sets the world record for women's flying speed at 181.18 miles per hour. Becomes vice president of public relations for New York–Philadelphia–Washington Airways (Ludington Line).
1931	Becomes first president of the Ninety-Nines. Marries George Palmer Putnam. Sets a women's autogiro altitude record of 18,415 feet and completes a transcontinental flight in an autogiro.
1932	Becomes the first woman and second person (after Charles Lindbergh) to fly solo across the Atlantic. Writes *The Fun of It*. Sets the women's record for the fastest nonstop transcontinental flight with a time of nineteen hours and five minutes. Becomes the first woman to fly solo across North America and back. Is awarded the Distinguished Flying Cross by Congress, France's Cross of the Knight of the Legion of Honor, the National Geographic Society's Gold Medal, and honorary membership in the National Aeronautic Association.

1933	Flies in the National Air Races. Breaks the transcontinental record with a time of seventeen hours, seven minutes, and thirty seconds. Awarded the Harmon Trophy.
1935	Becomes the first person to fly solo from Honolulu to Oakland, California. Flies solo from Los Angeles to Mexico City. Is the first woman to compete in the National Air Races.
1936	Becomes a women's career counselor at Purdue University. Purdue buys a Lockheed Model 10 Electra twin-engine airplane as a "flying laboratory."
1937	Attempts round-the-world flight that ends with a crash in Hawaii. The plane is repaired and she takes off again, this time from Miami. After nearly completing her round-the-world flight, disappears on her way to Howland Island on July 2.
1939	Is officially declared dead.

Earhart in an airplane, 1936.
Courtesy Library of Congress Prints and Photographs Division.

1.
On Flying Planes and Pilots

Amelia Earhart was only six when the Wright brothers achieved powered flight at Kitty Hawk. By the time she was twenty, military planes had revolutionized combat in World War I. When she was twenty-three, she went up in an airplane for the first time. She never wanted to come down.

When Earhart began flying during the 1920s, aviation was a dangerous male-dominated pursuit. Surplus wartime aircraft were used for barnstorming, which consisted of death-defying feats such as wing walking, jumping from plane to plane, death spirals, and dive-bombing crowds.[*]

Some pilots were pioneers. They vied to be the first to break a speed or endurance record like Charles Lindbergh, who was the first to fly solo across the Atlantic in 1927.

Though Earhart briefly considered stunt flying, her true interests were in pioneering and commercial aviation, all with an eye to opening up the skies to women. She flew planes, experimented

---

[*] Harrison, 105–21.

with parachutes, and was an early promoter of the autogiro, an aircraft with a rotating horizontal rotor for lift and an engine-propelled motor for thrust.

Flying was dangerous during the early part of the century. Gore Vidal, whose father was an aviation pioneer, remarked, "At least half of the people I used to see in my childhood would, suddenly, one day, not be there. 'Crashed' was the word; and nothing more was said."[*] Danger was a constant in Earhart's life, but she often appeared oblivious to it.

On Flying

Oh, Pidge, it's just like flying.[1]

Circa 1904; Earhart's declaration while riding
a homemade roller coaster at about age seven

I consider flying one of the sports and I think all persons, men and women, interested in sports, should participate in it.[2]

June 26, 1927, *Boston Daily Globe*

Not to have had a ride in an airplane today is like not having heard the radio.[3]

July 22, 1928, *Chicago Tribune*

I go wherever I please, or rather wherever I can land.[4]

October 10, 1928, *Omaha World Herald*

---

[*] Gore Vidal, "Love of Flying," *New York Review*, January 17, 1938, 18.

I have never asked any men to take a ride. I think I have always feared that some sense of gallantry would make them accept, even though they did not trust me. So my male passengers have always had to do the asking.[5]

Circa 1928

To those who haven't flown: "Fly."[6]

Circa 1928

Ours is the commencement of a flying age, and I am happy to have popped into existence at a period so interesting.[7]

Circa 1928

Flying is hard work. There is very little romance to it.[8]

March 3, 1929, *San Diego Union*

Try flying yourself. Probably you'll like it. At least you'll find it neither terrifying nor uncomfortable. And just by the mere act of going aloft—the open-mindedness of experimentation— you'll find yourself so much closer, I believe, to your boys and girls to whom flying, consciously or instinctively, is such an every-day matter.[9]

March 1929, *Hearst's International-Cosmopolitan*

As flying enters into everyday life, the dreams of centuries become actualities. One by one they take shape and become stepping-stones for other dreams.[10]

October 1929, *Hearst's International-Cosmopolitan*

People who inquire about air travel from me usually want to know only about the sensations they will encounter. I know I am going to hurt the feelings of certain individuals when I say there aren't any sensations to flying. Fiction writers so long have made romance and flying synonymous that too many imagine air travel is just one thrill after another, and little else.[11]

January 1931, *Hearst's International-Cosmopolitan*

You don't think of yourself when you're flying any more than you do in driving a car. You don't ask yourself in a traffic emergency, "Is my hat on straight?" You just think, "Can I get through that hole?" It's only the backseat drivers who have their minds on themselves. . . . You become a part of the machine.[12]

October 29, 1932, *Milwaukee Journal*

Flying is so much more than just a quick way to traverse space. It's freedom and color and form and style. I am at home in the air.[13]

February 7, 1934, *Christian Science Monitor*

The possibilities of flying haven't been touched.[14]

December 1, 1934, *Minneapolis Tribune*

People want to fly. The barrier is money. It still costs too much for the average person to buy a plane and fly it.[15]

Circa 1934–1935

The lure of flying is the lure of beauty. The dramas of the clouds, the glory of the stars, the charm of landscapes and the wonders of the waters and skies have, to me, an irresistible appeal.[16]

March 31, 1935, *Los Angeles Times*

Of course no pilot sits and feels his pulse as he flies. He has to be
part of the machine. If he thinks of anything but the task in
hand then trouble is probably just around the corner.[17]

Circa 1937

The last hour of an ocean flight is the hardest. I think all aviators who have flown over oceans feel the same thing. You constantly see mirages of land in the clouds that fade away nearly
as fast as they appear. You feel you are near land—
and imagination seems to do the rest.[18]

Date unknown

On the Thrill of Flight

Never use the word "thrill" in connection with aviation.
Aviators are not thrill seekers. They are men and women
interested in their work.[19]

Circa 1930–1937

Thrilled at flying? Oh, yes, of course, but not by the mere fact of flying. That gets to be a mechanical process just the same as driving a car. The real thrill, though, is in the gorgeous sights you see from a plane. . . . The greatest pleasure in aviation is an aesthetic one.[20]

October 29, 1932, *Milwaukee Journal*

Aviation is not thrilling according to what most people call
thrills. The first few flights, of course, are exhilarating, but after
that there is no more to it than riding in an automobile.[21]

February 1, 1933, *Oregon Journal* (Portland)

On Stunt Flying and Showmanship

For me flying was a sport and not a circus.[22]

Circa 1928

I should not advise any girl—or man, for that matter—to take up aviation for just the thrills and notoriety, or the money.[23]

Circa late 1920s

In flying, as in many modern pursuits, a certain amount of showmanship helps one to get over the rough spots—especially if flying is a profession and competition hard.[24]

Circa 1933

I cannot see what harm they do. Certainly their execution requires sturdy equipment and skill and determination on the part of the pilot. They may not point the way to progress in aviation but they demonstrate its possibilities. As for women's doing them, that probably will be necessary for some time—for contrary to legal precedent, they (women) are considered guilty of incompetence until proved otherwise.[25]

Circa 1933

On Airplanes

To my mind there is as much danger on a yacht as there is in an airplane.[26]

July 3, 1927, *Boston Herald*

I had rolled up the tremendous total of two and one-half hours' instruction when I decided that life was incomplete unless I owned my own plane.[27]

Circa 1928

I use my airplane like a family bus—to take me places.[28]

October 29, 1932, *Milwaukee Sentinel*

Airplanes are really still hand made. Too expensive. The price won't come down until enough people are actually making a move to fly, to create a demand the airplane manufacturers can translate into business.[29]

Circa 1934–1935

I don't see any sky flivver era for a while.[30]

March 30, 1935, *Minneapolis Star*. Flivvers were small, inexpensive cars, like the Model T Ford.

I feel that in any honor that might be accorded me, my plane should share the honors with me.[31]

Circa May 26, 1935

I have promised her that I will never ask her to make another record.... I shall turn her into green pastures. She has earned her rest. I do not believe, with her equipment, she could make any greater record than she has.[32]

June 7, 1935, *Atchison (KS) Daily Globe*; on her Lockheed Vega 5B

I'd like to find a tree on which new airplanes grow. I'd certainly shake myself down a good one.[33]

October 6, 1935, *St. Paul (MN) Pioneer Press*

My ambition is to have this wonderful gift produce practical results for the future of commercial flying and for the women who may want to fly tomorrow's planes.[34]

Circa July 1936; on her new Lockheed Electra 10E financed by Purdue University

I could write poetry about this ship.[35]

Circa 1936; on her Lockheed Electra 10E

It was a craft to delight the eye, its wings and fuselage painted red with gold stripes down the side. Possibly it may have seemed a trifle gaudy on the ground but I am sure it looked lovely against those white clouds.[36]

Circa 1937; reminiscing about her Lockheed Vega 5B

With the modern plane it seems to me that too often in the attainment of speed other considerations have been sacrificed. Safety, especially. Perhaps we would do well to go back to the elementary flying-machines of the early days and work forward from them all over again.[37]

Circa 1937

The pilot's prayer, I am sure, is not for more cunning and specialized instruments, but for a simplification of those existing.[38]

Circa 1937

If anyone had cause to lament, it was the Electra itself. For I put burdens upon her which in normal flying she was not built to bear. She carried a heavy overload. As a matter of fact, very few times since we started our partnership have I flown her without one.[39]

Circa 1937; on the crash of her Lockheed Electra 10E prior to the round-the-world flight

On the Autogiro

I hated to come down.[40]

April 9, 1931, *San Diego Union*; on her first experience flying as a passenger and, a few minutes later, as a pilot

So far as safety goes, the autogiro is the last word in airplanes.[41]

June 8, 1931, *Los Angeles Times*

The autogiro is a friendly airplane.[42]

July 19, 1931, *New York Times*

I am at a loss now to say whether I flew it or it flew me.[43]

August 1931, *Hearst's International-Cosmopolitan*

The autogiro will never be practical for transport purposes. Its main advantage, of course, is that it does facilitate landing in very small spaces.[44]

December 1, 1935, *Zanesville (OH) Signal*

On Parachutes

This was more fun than a roller coaster.[45]

Circa June 1935; on her first parachute jump

I've never had to use a parachute in my own flying, but I suppose the day comes for all of us.[46]

Date unknown

On Pilots

Not all people can fly, any more than all can or should drive motor cars.[47]

January 1929, *Hearst's International-Cosmopolitan*.

When you see a pilot dance you can tell if he or she is a good pilot. A good pilot will betray the rhythmic coordination of a good dancer, that unconscious balance and freedom of motion.[48]

Circa 1930–1937

Aviators are not a race apart, gloriously different and removed from other people.[49]

Circa 1930–1937

It doesn't take any more prowess to be a super-flyer than it does to be a super something else.[50]

Circa 1933

There are slim ones and plump ones and quiet ones and those who talk all the time. They're large and small, young and old, and half the list are married and many of these have children. In a word, they are simply thoroughly normal girls and women who happen to have taken up flying rather than golf, swimming or steeplechasing.[51]

Circa 1933; on women pilots

There should be rigorous tests. Those that pass such tests will be competent to fly planes.[52]

May 2, 1935, *Boston Daily Globe*; advocating pilot licenses

If there is any time when experience counts it is in putting down the temptation to wander from that course which instruments declare is true to that which the human mind would like to try. A pilot's maxim should be, "Usually the instruments are right and you are wrong."[53]

May 1935, *National Geographic*

Pilots are always dreaming dreams.[54]

Circa 1937

Pilots love to fly because of the beauty of flight— whether they know it or not.[55]

Date unknown

On Women as Pilots

Some day women will fly the Atlantic and think little of it because it is an ordinary thing to do.[56]

June 21, 1928, *Times* (London)

One thing disturbs me—a little—and that is the way some people seem to think a woman who crosses the Atlantic by air has something abnormal about her; some strange characteristic that a man who flew the Atlantic would not have. There really is not anything so amazing in liking to fly, or in flying anywhere any more. The amazing thing is that so few women, seeing what sport men are having in the air, are having it themselves.[57]

June 22, 1928, *New York Times*

I am lonesome for the companionship of women in aviation. . . . When I want to "talk shop" in aviation at home there are only men to talk to.[58]

June 22, 1928, *New York Times*

Women should realize that really any woman who can drive a motorcar can learn to pilot an airplane.[59]

July 6, 1928, *Christian Science Monitor*

The field is clear for the pioneer and if the pioneer has good ideas nobody will ask whether the pioneer is a man or a woman.[60]

Circa 1928

How is a fellow going to earn spurs without at least trying to ride?[61]

June 12, 1929, *New York Times*; Earhart's reaction to the National Aeronautic Association's requirement that female pilots fly with a male navigator. The association dropped the rule.

There is no cause inherent in her nature which would make a woman inferior to a man as an air pilot.[62]

July 30, 1929, *New York Times*

At the present time there is a certain prejudice against employing women in flying capacities, which considering their experience, is not unreasonable. . . . Some of the women who cry loudest about prejudice would not venture into an airplane flown by one of their less experienced sisters.[63]

July 1929, *Hearst's International-Cosmopolitan*

I am not urging the employment of unqualified women in the aviation industry. All I hope is that those who have ability and who get adequate training by some means, will be given a chance to make a living as pilots, *if they wish to*.[64]

July 1929, *Hearst's International-Cosmopolitan*

Still [girls and women] are being retarded. But the pendulum is swinging. Women are determined to be an integral part of aviation. Speed the day when the announcement is made of the first aviation training school "exclusively for girls."[65]

October 26, 1929, *Literary Digest*

Sooner or later the big airlines must enlist women's intelligent cooperation, because without them aviation cannot hope for success. One only has to study the history of the automobile industry to recognize the truth of what I am saying.[66]

October 26, 1929, *Literary Digest*

Knowledge concerning the air, the plane and the pilot should be the possession of every intelligent woman.[67]

May 1930, *Needlecraft: The Magazine of Home Arts*

Nearly half the women aviators I know are married. They manage to coordinate their family life and business life very well. Some of them have sweet little children.[68]

July 15, 1930, *Seattle Daily Times*

The feminists of aviation are doing a great deal of harm by taking credit which doesn't belong to them, by having their pictures taken in front of planes they can't fly.[69]

August 14, 1930, *Boston Daily Globe*

There is no reason why woman can't hold any position in aviation providing she can overcome prejudices and show ability.[70]

May 9, 1931, *New York Times*

You must remember women haven't had access to the military equipment which made possible the establishment of the world altitude record. They have made these records in spite of handicaps.[71]

July 26, 1931, *San Diego Union*

I hope women keep on trying to enter aviation. In doing so they must overcome what they have had to in any business and do twice as well as men to get half the credit.[72]

Circa November 1931

It doesn't matter much who flies it. Men or women; it's all the same.[73]

May 24, 1932, *Florence (AL) Times*

I have gone up with a mechanic who doesn't know the controls from the altimeter and when I've come down I've heard people say he probably did most of the flying. So I determined to show them.[74]

May 24, 1932, *Boston Daily Globe*. By flying the Atlantic solo, Earhart proved that she was a capable pilot.

In aviation, the Department of Commerce recognizes no legal difference between men and women licensed to fly. I feel that similar equality should be carried to all fields of endeavor.[75]

September 23, 1932, *Spokane (WA) Daily Chronicle*

Aviation is just as much a woman's job as it is a man's and I'll admit it is a pretty big one for me, but I still find time to devote to married life.[76]

December 15, 1932, *McKeesport (PA) Daily News*

There are no women pilots in the cockpits of any of the scheduled airplanes today. This is partly due to prejudice, and partly due to the fact that women have more difficulty in learning the rudiments of flying than men. The Army and Navy training is not open to them; they must pay for all the instruction they get . . . and it is not only hard for a woman to get instruction, but also to get experience.[77]

January 23, 1933, *The Campus* (Sarah Lawrence College, Bronxville, NY)

The next great achievement for women in flying does not lie in the direction of the spectacular, but in attaining their place in the regularly-scheduled air lines as pilots and mechanics—establishing their place in the industry on an equality with men.[78]

February 4, 1933, *Vancouver (BC) Daily Province*

Tradition has been a terrible handicap for women. Sometimes I think tradition is the hardest obstacle we have to fight. I actually know men and women who not only are surprised that I can fly, but are surprised that women can do anything interesting.[79]

June 30, 1933, *New York Telegram*

We hope that women pilots will soon be regarded as "pilots" and not as "women pilots."[80]

September 26, 1933, *Boston Daily Globe*. They were also called Ladybirds, Angels, and Sweethearts of the Air.

Heredity hampers most women flyers. We've been brought up to scream at the sight of a mouse. Fears of that sort are not the best thing for a woman who plans to fly. But I think considerable progress in aviation has been made recently by women.[81]

November 22, 1933, *Times Union* (Albany, NY)

Some day, I dare say, women can be flyers and yet not regarded as curiosities.[82]

Circa 1933

Now and then, girls marry into flying and become wives of men who can and do teach them. This is one way to get coveted lessons, but probably not advisable unless the gentlemen in question possess other charms in addition to being good instructors.[83]

Circa 1933. Earhart may have been referring to Anne Morrow Lindbergh, whose husband taught her to fly. Earhart admired Anne but was appalled by how she was treated by Charles.[84]

In aviation as a whole, women are outnumbered forty to one, but I feel that more will gain admittance as a greater number knock at the door. If and when you knock at the door, *it might be well to bring an ax along; you may have to chop your way through*.[85]

1934 speech entitled "Choosing a Career"

I believe that eventually women flyers will be considered solely on their abilities as pilots. If a woman wishes to enter important competitions the question will be "Is she a good enough flyer?" instead of primarily a matter or whether she wears skirts or trousers.[86]

September 8, 1936, *Los Angeles Times*

We women pilots have a rough, rocky road ahead of us. Each accomplishment, no matter how small, is important. Although it may be no direct contribution to the science of aeronautics nor its technical development, it will encourage other women to fly. The more women who fly, the more women become pilots, the q uicker we will be recognized as an important factor in aviation.[87]

Circa 1937

[I want] recognition for women. Men do not believe us capable. We can fly—you know that. Ever since we started we've batted our heads against a stone wall. Manufacturers refuse us planes. The public have no confidence in our ability. If we had access to the equipment and training men have, we could certainly do as well. Thank heaven, we continue willingly fighting a losing battle. Every year we pour thousands of dollars into flight training with no hope of return. A man can work his way through flight training or he can join the army. When he has a license he can obtain a flying job to build up his time. A man can borrow the latest equipment for specialized flights or for records; and what do we get? Obsolete airplanes. And why? Because we are women; seldom are we trusted to do an efficient job . . . but if enough of us keep trying, we'll get someplace.[88]

Circa 1937

Women must pay for everything. They do get more glory than men for comparable feats, but, they also get more notoriety when they crash.[89]

Date unknown

Young Earhart in flying gear, circa 1922.
Courtesy Purdue University Libraries, Archives and Special Collections.

2.
On Earhart's Own Flights

Earhart very nearly wasn't the first woman to cross the Atlantic. American Mabel Boll and German Thea Rasche were both in Newfoundland waiting for the right weather conditions at the same time as Earhart.[*] In the end, the *Friendship*, piloted by Wilmer Stultz and Louis Gordon, departed first. It was expected that Earhart, as a licensed aviator, would briefly pilot the plane, but weather conditions made that inadvisable. Instead she was written in the history books as a passenger.

As a result of the flight, Earhart achieved instant fame on both sides of the Atlantic. When she returned to the United States, she was regarded as a conquering hero and was met with parades and dinner at the White House as a guest of President Calvin Coolidge. All this was despite the fact that she did not pilot the plane. In every conversation, every interview, she awarded credit to Stultz and Gordon, as well as Amy Guest, who had financed the flight.

---

[*] Lovell, 112–17.

Still, it stung when a British feminist magazine decried that she was "carried, as a bundle might be carried, across the Atlantic."[*]

As a result, in 1932, when Earhart planned to fly the Atlantic again, it was to be a solo flight. She hoped to match Charles Lindbergh's dangerous 1927 crossing.

In the years following Lindbergh, many others tried. In 1927 alone, nineteen men and women died in the attempt.[†] American Ruth Elder crashed in the ocean, but she was picked up by a passing ship and survived.[‡] Frances Grayson, a niece of President Woodrow Wilson's, disappeared on her transatlantic attempt.[§] Earhart's friend Ruth Nichols took off in June 1931 but broke her back when she crash-landed in Canada.[¶]

So when Earhart flew the ocean and landed in a pasture in Ireland on May 31, 1932, she defied the odds. She didn't fly as far as Lindbergh, who had landed in Paris, but she did feel that she had earned her place in the history books.

When Earhart married George Putnam in 1931 (see chapter 11 for more on their relationship), many assumed her flying career was over. Upon marriage, women of her generation were expected to quit their jobs and become housewives. Earhart was an exception. She continued her work as a pilot, a promoter of personal and commercial flight, and an advocate of vocations for women.

---

[*] "Feminists Dislike Earhart Welcome," unknown publication, Earhart scrapbook 3, AESB003, GPPC.
[†] Brady, 374.
[‡] Lawrence, 95.
[§] Johnson, 71.
[¶] Butler, 256–57.

After her solo transatlantic flight, Earhart continued to participate in air derbies, set records, and make groundbreaking flights. She flew solo from Hawaii to Oakland, California, was the first person to fly solo from Los Angeles to Mexico City, and then flew from Mexico City to Newark.

Earhart was not yet forty when she took off for her round-the-world flight. It was a voyage fraught with extreme challenges such as pilot and navigator fatigue, the unreliability of fuel supplies, problems with maps and celestial navigation, and the possibility of landing in hostile territories.

She crashed on her initial attempt. Months of repairs resulted in a change of route. Instead of beginning with the longest stretch, from Hawaii to Asia, they would take on that segment at the end of their journey, when they were most fatigued. Further, they had to locate and land on Howland Island, a coral island barely two miles long in the middle of the Pacific. Earhart was last heard from on July 2, 1937.

On Her First Flights as a Passenger

My first airplane flight . . . delighted me so much that I was determined, on the moment, not to rest until I had learned to fly, myself.[1]

August 1932, *American Magazine*

By the time I was 200 feet in the air, I knew I must learn to be a pilot.[2]

December 7, 1933, *Dallas Morning News*

On Her Transatlantic Crossing of June 1928

I don't wish it to be inferred that this flight is in any way a race with Mabel Boll. Our flight is being carried on independent of any other.[3]

June 8, 1928, *Washington Post*. Beating Boll was precisely the goal of the *Friendship* crew.

I'm the proudest woman in the world.[4]

June 18, 1928, *Rochester (NY) Evening Journal*

I did not know if we were in England, Wales or Ireland. But I did know that I was the first woman to fly the Atlantic and my heart was in my mouth with excitement.[5]

June 19, 1928, *Morning Star* (Rockford, IL)

Perhaps some people have been thinking that this was just another "stunt" flight, but it was not. We have come to a stage in aviation where the need is technical advancement more than spectacular stunts.[6]

June 20, 1928, *Times* (London)

Because I love life and all it has to offer. I want every opportunity and adventure it can give.[7]

June 20, 1928, *New York Sun*; on why she flew the Atlantic.

It really makes me a little resentful that the mere fact that I am a woman apparently overshadows the tremendous feat of flying that Bill Stultz has accomplished.[8]

June 21, 1928, *Boston Herald*

Out of this flight, one idea has become crystallized: that it must be made possible for women to become as much interested in aviation as for men.[9]

July 6, 1928, *Christian Science Monitor*

Please forget I am a woman. I didn't think about it flying the Atlantic.[10]

July 7, 1928, *Cleveland Plain Dealer*

I was lucky to be chosen to fly with these two men. It was a great journey and I am proud I was the girl.[11]

July 7, 1928, *Cleveland Plain Dealer*

It was not courageous of me at all to fly the ocean, it was just my vacation. If we have succeeded in furthering the interests of aviation, I am glad.[12]

July 8, 1928, *Cleveland Plain Dealer*

I suppose we should have had interesting thoughts about our friends and homes of the past or our thrills of future success. But so great was our concentration on the task at hand that I doubt if any of our minds did more than run around in circles that concentrated on weather and speed and the always present hope that when morning came we could at last see land.[13]

July 12, 1928, *Los Angeles Times*

I was just baggage.[14]

July 26, 1928, *Evening Repository* (Canton, OH)

It was an experience in a pioneering adventure that would lure anyone. An experience whose chief importance lay not merely in the excitement of the enterprise itself, but because the flight, we hope, may prove a milestone in aviation progress, and a pointer, at least, on the high-road of women's participation in flying.[15]

October 1928, *McCall's*

The opportunity came as casually as an invitation to the matinee, and it came by telephone.[16]

Circa 1928

At first I thought the conversation was a joke, and told the gentleman so. At least twice before I had been approached by bootleggers.[17]

Circa 1928. During Prohibition, pilots were sought to ferry illegal liquor.

If I were found wanting on too many counts I would be deprived of the trip. On the other hand, if I were just too fascinating the gallant gentlemen might be loath to drown me.[18]

Circa 1928

Essentially this was a feminine expedition, organized and financed by a woman, whose wish was to emphasize what her sex stood ready to do.[19]

Circa 1928; on Lady Amy Phipps Guest's sponsorship of the flight

Here is where Atlantic flights by women, or any other good flight helps—it starts women to think.[20]

Circa 1928

> Two musketeers and—what is a female musketeer?[21]

Circa 1928; on Gordon, Stultz, and herself

> As to the part I personally played in the flight, I have tried to be entirely frank always. The credit belongs to the boys, to the ship, and to its backer. I was a passenger. The fact that I happened to be a small-ship pilot, reasonably experienced in the air, didn't affect the situation otherwise than having contributed to my selection.[22]

Circa 1931

> My flight added nothing to aviation.[23]

October 25, 1933, *Morning Star* (Rockford, IL)

On the Women's Air Derby of 1929

> If we can't fly the race and navigate our own course through the Rockies, I for one, won't enter.[24]

June 12, 1929, *New York Times*. Earhart and other female flyers refused to accept National Aeronautic Association plans to shorten the women's course or to require women to have navigators. They were allowed to fly solo.

> Marvel Crosson left a challenge to the women of the derby and there is certainly no aftermath of fear among us.[25]

Circa August 1929; reaction to the death of fellow flyer Marvel Crosson

On Her Solo Transatlantic Crossing of 1932

> Would you *mind* if I flew the Atlantic?[26]

Circa early 1932; question posed to her husband, George Putnam

I've come from America.[27]

May 21, 1932; greeting to Dan McCallion, a startled Irish dairy farmer, upon landing in his pasture. His reply: "Do ye be tellin' me that now?"

There is no comparison. On this go I was flying low the whole time and had to rely on myself.[28]

May 21, 1932, *Christian Science Monitor*

It was a terrifying and a thrilling experience— the most thrilling I have ever had. But, I'd do it again.[29]

May 22, 1932, *The American*

I did this just for fun.[30]

May 22, 1932, *Boston Herald*

I made my flight partly in the spirit of adventure, but also to justify my previous flight.[31]

May 23, 1932, *Northern Whig and Belfast Post*

I flew the Atlantic because I though it was time some woman should do it.[32]

June 3, 1932, *Telegraph* (Nashua, NH)

I think, that the appreciation of the deed is out of proportion to the deed itself. . . . I shall be happy if my small exploit has drawn attention to the fact that women, too, are flying.[33]

June 21, 1932; response to praise by President Herbert Hoover

If it means something to women in aviation, to help in the struggle to show that women are capable of taking a place beside men in aeronautics, my effort has been justified.[34]

June 21, 1932, *New York Herald Tribune*

Some features of the flight I fear have been exaggerated. It made a much better story to say I landed with but one gallon of gasoline left. As a matter of fact, I had more than a hundred. The exact quantity I remember because I had to pay a tax for every gallon imported into Ireland![35]

June 21, 1932

It was a consummation of my desire to wipe out the idea that I was just a "sack of potatoes" on the *Friendship* trip.[36]

June 30, 1932, *Boston Daily Globe*

My particular inner desire to fly the Atlantic alone was nothing new with me. I had flown Atlantics before. Everyone has his own Atlantics to fly. Whatever you want very much to do, against the opposition of tradition, neighborhood opinion, and so-called "common sense"—that is an Atlantic.[37]

August 1932, *American Magazine*

I had been on the sidelines when I wanted to play the game itself. . . . I wanted to justify myself to myself. I wanted to prove that I deserved at least a small fraction of the nice things said about me. . . . I already had the credit—heaped up and running over.[38]

August 1932, *American Magazine*; reflecting on how being "baggage" in 1928 induced her solo Atlantic flight

I did no regretting and, indeed, precious little worrying. The project involved a gamble, but gambling is a human frailty, and I suppose there is a certain extra fascination in playing for high stakes. The stake in this throw, of course, was my life against the joy of doing something I wanted to do very much.[39]

September 1932, *Hearst's International-Cosmopolitan*

I did not kill a cow in landing—unless one died of fright.[40]

September 1932, *National Geographic*

There was no use turning back, for I knew I couldn't land at Harbor Grace in the dark even if I could find my way. And I didn't want to roll up in a ball with all that gasoline. . . . So it seemed sensible to keep going.[41]

Circa 1932; regarding equipment failures on the flight, including a broken altimeter and a fire in one engine

I figured I had one chance in 10 of succeeding.[42]

December 12, 1933, *Omaha World Herald*

On Her Transcontinental Flight from Los Angeles to Newark

Don't come near me. If you knew what I feel like.[43]

August 26, 1932, *Boston Daily Globe*. Reporters assumed Earhart was ill. But in addition to being exhausted, she likely reeked of urine. Female flyers were often unable to use relief tubes designed for men.*

---

* Rich, 145–46.

On the 1933 National Air Races

It does not matter much whether the women flyers will make good records. At least we shall have entered the race and that will open the way for other girls next year and all the years after that.[44]

June 30, 1933, *New York Telegram*. Earhart and Ruth Nichols, the only female entrants, came in fifth and sixth respectively.

On the 1935 National Air Races (Bendix Trophy)

I don't think I have much chance of winning in this whip, but I am going for the ride anyway.[45]

August 31, 1935, *Rochester (NY) Journal*. Earhart came in fifth.

We had no more intention of going than you, but we got to figuring pilots' chances and decided we would win fifth place against ships 50–90 miles faster than Lockheed. So we cranked up and cruised along and won $500. Enough to pay our expenses. We had fun. Old Bessie the fire horse came through.[46]

September 4, 1935; letter to her mother

On Her 1935 Flight from Hawaii to California

It's easier to hit a continent than an island.[47]

Circa autumn 1934; on why she flew from Hawaii to California and not vice versa

> To have a hand in helping to bring closer together such important parts of the United States as Hawaii and the mainland is something I would always be proud of.[48]

December 22, 1934, *Los Angeles Times*

> Unwarranted criticism which has been leveled at me and my flight plans. As you know the barrage of belittlement has made harder the preparation, in many ways. So malicious does some of it seem that I suggest you search for evidence of sabotage in case of an unexplained mishap.
>
> I make the attempt to fly from Honolulu to the mainland of my own free will. I am familiar with the hazards.... If I do not do a good job it will not be because of the plane and motor are not excellent nor because women cannot fly.[49]

January 8, 1935; letter to her husband

> The entire responsibility for the flight I assume.[50]

January 10, 1935; letter to Major Earnest C. Clark, absolving the army of responsibility if she failed.

> To me, also, it seemed good training for other hoped-for long-distance flights.[51]

January 13, 1935, *New York Times*

> I wanted to escape the fuss and crowds of a preannounced departure. It was easier to have no "Aloha."[52]

January 13, 1935, *New York Times*; on why she did not announce her departure time from Hawaii

The greatest hazard I had to overcome was the criticism heaped on my head for even contemplating the flight. For this reason it was infinitely more difficult than my two Atlantic flights.[53]

January 13, 1935, *New York Times*

Gentlemen, there is an aroma of cowardice in the air. You know as well as I do that the rumor is trash, but if you can be intimidated, it might as well be true. Whether you live in fear or defend your integrity is your decision. I have made mine. I intend to fly to California within this next week, with or without your support.[54]

Circa January 1935. Hawaiian agricultural interests threatened to withdraw $10,000 of funding following criticism that their support was a ploy to persuade the government to reduce sugar taxes.

I am getting tired of this fog.[55]

May 1935, *National Geographic*. Earhart transmitted this message, but only "I'm tired" was heard, promoting concern that she was seriously fatigued and would not succeed.

I *was* glad to see land—but not in a state to "scream for joy," as reported in one fervid account. My faithful plane, I believe, would fall apart under me if its pilot grew so senselessly emotional.[56]

May 1935, *National Geographic*

A special mental hazard was the sight of three fire engines and an ambulance in front of the hangar.[57]

August 10, 1935, *Chautauqua (NY) Daily*

On Her 1935 Flight to Mexico, Then to Newark, New Jersey

It's silly that a bug caused me to fail, but I intend to return and make a perfect flight.[58]

April 21, 1935, *New York Times*. Earhart claimed that an insect caused her unplanned landing in Nopala, Hidalgo, Mexico, thus interrupting what she hoped to be a nonstop journey.

It was really not a particularly interesting flight.[59]

May 9, 1935, *New York Times*. This contradicts her saying, "From a pilot's standpoint it was an interesting journey."[60]

Contrasted to the Atlantic crossing, that was a journey of stars, not storms; of tropic loveliness instead of ice.[61]

Circa 1937

And Wiley Post, who had voluntarily braved every sort of flying hazard, said to me, "AE, don't do it. It's too dangerous." That was challenging.[62]

Unknown date. Wiley Post was a friend and a famous aviator.

On Her 1937 Round-the-World Flight

The rumor about the world flight in June is applesauce. . . . It would take months to prepare such a trip—maybe in a year.[63]

April 1, 1936; letter from Earhart to her mother. Despite her denial, Earhart's planned flight was public knowledge.

No one has ever landed at Howland. It is a coral island. . . .
I hope to land there.[64]

February 12, 1937, *Christian Science Monitor*

[To satisfy] the ego that everyone exhibits sooner or later.[65]

March 7, 1937, *Los Angeles Times*; on her reason for the flight

It's funny. I'm not at all frightened.[66]

March 12, 1937, *San Francisco Chronicle*

It would be foolhardy for me to try to fly the Pacific without an experienced navigator.[67]

March 18, 1937, *Christian Science Monitor*. Many assumed that Earhart would fly solo around the world and were surprised when she chose Fred Noonan as navigator.

I wouldn't go so far as to say there is a real need to blaze a trail around the earth's equator—but every flight of this kind, pioneering, I mean, has actual value to the future of aviation.[68]

March 18, 1937, *Christian Science Monitor*

No one is hurt, only our spirits are bruised. This means postponement of my world trip, but not cancellation.[69]

March 20, 1937, *Christian Science Monitor*; on her plane crash in Hawaii

If we don't burn up, I want to try again.[70]

Circa March 20, 1937; Earhart's thoughts on the crash

I have a feeling that there is just about one more good flight left in my system and I hope this trip around the world is it. Anyway, when I have finished this job, I mean to give up long-distance stunt flying.... I'm getting old and want to make way for the younger generation before I'm feeble too.[71]

Circa March 1937; interview with Carl Allen

So I am more or less mortgaging the future to go on. But what are futures for?[72]

April 12, 1937, *Boston Daily Globe*

I am going for fun. Can you think of a better reason?[73]

May 30, 1937, *New York Times*

Very confidentially I may hop off in a few days. I am going to try to beat the newspapers. So you don't know nothin'.[74]

Circa May 1937; letter to her mother

I know that if I fail or if I am lost you will be blamed for allowing me to leave on this trip; the backers of the flight will be blamed and everyone connected with it. But it's my responsibility and mine alone.[75]

Circa May 1937; letter to her husband

I'm not taking any risks but am flying as fast as possible. From Lae to Howland Island, 1,550 miles, will be the worst section of the flight, but with Freddy Noonan navigating, I'm confident we'll make it.[76]

June 28, 1937, *Portsmouth (OH) Times*

Gas fumes in plane from fueling made me sick again this morning after starting. Stomach getting weak I guess.[77]

Circa June 1937. Some speculate that Earhart was pregnant, while others ascribe her discomfort to gas fumes and dysentery.[78]

It's been a grand trip. We'll do it again, together, some time.[79]

Circa June 1937; phone conversation between Earhart in Karachi and George Putnam in New York

Not much more than a month ago I was on the other shore of the Pacific, looking westward. This evening, I looked eastward over the Pacific. In those fast-moving days which have intervened, the whole width of the world has passed behind us—except this broad ocean. I shall be glad when we have the hazards of its navigation behind us.[80]

Circa late June 1937

KHAQQ calling *Itasca*. We must be on you but cannot see you but gas is running low. Been unable to reach you by radio.[81]

June 30, 1937. KHAQQ was Earhart's call sign. She signaled to the US Coast Guard cutter *Itasca*.

At Darwin, by the way, we left the parachutes we had carried that far, to be shipped home. A parachute would not help over the Pacific.[82]

Circa 1937

I've wanted to do this flight for a long time. . . . I've worked hard and I deserve *one* fling during my lifetime.[83]

Circa 1937

Here was shining adventure, beckoning with new experiences, added knowledge of flying, of peoples—of myself.[84]

Circa 1937

Please know I am quite aware of the hazards. I want to do it because I want to do it. Women must try to do things as men have tried. When they fail their failure must be but a challenge to others.[85]

Circa 1937

Please don't be concerned. It just seems that I must try this flight. I've weighed it carefully. With it behind me life will be fuller and richer. I can be content. Afterward it will be fun to grow old.[86]

Circa 1937; conversation with her husband

As for this present venture, I just want to progress as safely and sanely as day-to-day conditions make possible, give myself and the Electra the experience of seeing what we can of this very interesting world at its waistline and, with good fortune, get back with plane and pilot all "in one piece."[87]

Circa 1937

It is only fair to record that the Bureau of Aeronautics probably would have preferred that I abandon the effort. Its policy was to discourage extracurricular undertakings of this kind, the common or garden term for something which is "stunt flights." But having granted me permission once, the ship, personnel and flight plan being the same, it would have been difficult to withdraw it.[88]

Circa 1937. The Bureau of Aeronautics gave its approval despite the crash on her first attempt.

"*Push through.*" I find myself writing those words almost resentfully. We're always pushing through, hurrying on our long way, trying to get to some other place instead of enjoying the place we'd already got to. A situation, alas, about which there was no use complaining. I'd made my schedule and had to abide by it.[89]

Circa 1937

On Her Accidents

I did what I thought was best in the circumstances.[90]

June 6, 1931; on a Tulsa, Oklahoma, autogiro crash. Though reprimanded by the Department of Commerce, she insisted that she had crashed because she was trying to avoid a crowd.

I under-estimated the distance. Possibly a whirlwind caught the tail of the autogyro.[91]

June 12, 1931, *Evening Tribune* (San Diego); on an accident in Abilene, Texas, that damaged three cars

The reprimand wasn't one really, mostly a chore for letting the Ludington line and I the goat. I am not a careless pilot and the letter doesn't say so.[92]

Circa July 1931; letter to her mother regarding a reprimand from the Commerce Department after the Abilene autogiro accident

GP fell over a wire running to pick me up and as he limped up I said, "It was all my fault," meaning that he was hurt. The papers got it I said the crack [up] was mine which isn't accurate.[93]

September 17, 1931; letter to her mother. Earhart was uninjured in the autogiro accident. George Putnam required medical attention after tripping.

So, flying is the safest—after all! If you'd been with me, you wouldn't have been hurt.[94]

Circa September 1931; remark made to her husband after he tripped

You know, Ruth, I always feel that you have to take some chances on long-distance flights, so I don't bother to go into all the possible accidents that might happen. I just don't think about crackups.[95]

Circa 1932; conversation with Ruth Nichols prior to her solo transatlantic flight

We had the accident at Honolulu simply because I was asking the heavily-overloaded plane to do more than it ever was supposed to do.[96]

March 26, 1937, *Los Angeles Times*; on the Electra crash on her first attempt at a round-the-world flight

On Her Records

Don't tempt me; you wait.[97]

July 8, 1928, *Boston Daily Globe*. Flying the Atlantic on the *Friendship* whetted Earhart's appetite for more records.

Today I think I broke the women's speed record in average time of 184.^{17} m.p.h. I did one loop in 197+.[98]

November 22, 1929; letter to her mother

I think I can do better than that.[99]

April 9, 1931, *New York Times*; on setting a record for 19,000 feet in an autogiro

Records as such may or may not be important, but at least the more of them women make, the more forcefully it is demonstrated that they can and do fly. Directly or indirectly, more opportunities for those who wish to enter the aviation world should be opened by such evidence.[100]

Circa 1933

Earhart with arms spread in front of her plane, February 12, 1937.
Courtesy Purdue University Libraries, Archives and Special Collections.

3.
On the Aviation Industry

In 1918 the United States government began official airmail routes.[*] Airmail proved profitable, and carriers weren't interested in flying passengers because they made six times more money carrying mail.[†] For its part, the American public wasn't particularly interested in flying either. Turbulence, exhaust fumes, and airsickness were common. As one official described, "People were so sick they used rubber matting instead of carpeting on the floor of the plane.... They used to say passengers didn't get out of a plane, they slid out—skated down the aisle."[‡]

Commercial aviation promoters hoped to change their image. Following her first transatlantic crossing, Amelia Earhart was constantly asked her opinions on aviation, and thus she became a de facto spokesperson for the industry. Her enthusiasm and professionalism soon resulted in job offers. First she was hired by

---
[*] Crouch, 207.
[†] Brady, 172.
[‡] Rich, 107.

Transcontinental Air Transport, where her job was to promote flying among women.[*] A year later she was employed by the Ludington Line, which offered a commuter service to New York, Philadelphia, and Washington, DC. Though the company eventually failed, its high proportion of female passengers—about half—was testimony to Earhart's influence.[†]

Earhart's last commercial venture was an offshoot of the Boston and Maine Railroad. It offered flights between Boston, Massachusetts, and Bangor, Waterville, and Portland, Maine. Earhart organized large-scale public events where influential women took to the air—most for the first time.[‡] Although Earhart put her all into promoting commercial aviation, it would be another two decades before passenger flight truly achieved commercial success.

> Aviation is a great thing, but it cannot fill one's life completely.[1]
>
> June 20, 1928, *New York Times*

> Certainly, it is reasonable to foresee that "airway" will win in our language as definite a place as "railway" or "highway."[2]
>
> March 1929, *Hearst's International-Cosmopolitan*

> Aviation is transportation—it is no longer in the experimental or circus stunting stage.[3]
>
> May 20, 1930, Chicago newspaper

---

[*] Ware, 66.
[†] Van Pelt, 107.
[‡] "Over 200 Women Take to Air over Augusta as Guests of Noted Aviatrix Amelia Earhart," *Kennebec Journal* (Augusta, ME), August 15, 1934

If I had a grandmother who wished to go from one coast to the other, I should certainly send her on what I considered the best airline, confident of it's [sic] being the most comfortable way for her to go. Not only would she avoid several fatiguing days and nights of train travel, but she would have unexcelled personal service. Further, if I wished to take children—even small ones—on the same journey, I should go by air.[4]

January 1931, *Hearst's International-Cosmopolitan*

Mothers should always go with their children when the children take their first airplane rides. The children are going to fly anyway, and if forbidden they'll take cheap rides in unlicensed planes and incur a risk.[5]

March 8, 1931, *New York Times*

I use my plane exactly as I use my car. That is why I believe that aviation is as practical for women as for me.[6]

November 15, 1932, *Williams Record* (Williams College, Williamstown, MA)

We who are interested in aviation would like to have it regarded just as any other industry. We don't want people to feel that it is strange or exotic. It is a form of transportation necessary to business and industry, and should be treated as such.[7]

January 23, 1933, *The Campus* (Sarah Lawrence College, Bronxville, NY)

Aviation isn't romantic, it's work. It's as much of an industry as the railroads or making automobiles or lumbering. Romance, no; it's plain hard work.[8]

February 2, 1933, *Oregonian* (Portland)

Aviation has grown up, you know. It isn't a plaything any more. It has become a serious and useful industry, taking its place in modern life much the same as other forms of transportation—the railroad and the ocean liner for example.[9]

June 1933, *Screenland*

No other phase of modern progress continues to maintain such a brimming measure of romance and beauty coupled with utility as does aviation.[10]

Circa 1935; radio address

To the modern child, girl or boy, there is no great wonder in aviation. It is as routine to them as the automobile is to their parents, whose parents in turn saw the automobile replace horse-drawn vehicles, many no doubt rebelling at the innovation and the inherent "dangers" of gasoline propulsion.[11]

February 13, 1937, *Liberty*

In aviation, talking before one has anything to talk about is poor policy.[12]

Circa 1937

Aviation is a serious, sane, dependable and prosaic business, and not a spectacular and romantic adventure.[13]

Date unknown

Aviation is just another friendly business; and there are sixty other business enterprises vitally associated with it. It is not a business that has come to take the place of rail, steamship or automobile transportation, but to take a place with these other equally modern modes of travel. And there is room for them all in this day and age.[14]

Date unknown

Probably no field presents greater lure for young people—explorers—than aviation. It has the color and movement of flying to kindle the imagination, and its growing importance as an industry is tempting to those who plan serious careers in transportation, for aviation is simply the newest form of transportation—the climax of the pageant of human progress from oxcart to airplane.[15]

Date unknown

On Aviation in the United States

We are behind the rest of the flying world in commercial aviation, and every woman should do her share.[16]

July 8, 1928, *Boston Daily Globe*

No country is ahead of America in flying.[17]

December 1, 1932, *Erie (PA) Daily Times*

On Aviation and the Government

Abroad, the entire industry is generously subsidized by the various governments. Of course, aviation, here knows no such support, a fact which means that, so far as we have gone, our industry is on a sound basis economically.[18]

Circa 1928

Aviation should not be restricted too much until its maturity is reached. The industry is still young and it should not be killed before it develops.[18]

March 20, 1934, *Register-Republican* (Rockford, IL)

On the Future of Aviation

With very fast airplanes there may be a vast commuting system built up which will permit city workers to live a hundred or two hundred miles from the office and yet be no farther away in time than at present.[19]

October 1929, *Hearst's International-Cosmopolitan*

Airports may be connected by tubes to the centers of population so the loss of time to outlying sections may be eliminated. There may be central landing fields on train sheds or buildings where passengers will disembark, leaving the airplane to return to a more distant field for hangar facilities.[20]

October 1929, *Hearst's International-Cosmopolitan*

It's possible the autogiros will be rubbing shoulders with automobiles in our garage-hangars of tomorrow.[21]

August 1931, *Hearst's International-Cosmopolitan*

> I believe transatlantic air travel will sometime be as regular and reliable as railroad traffic today.[22]

June 18, 1932, *Christian Science Monitor*

> We will see commercial planes crossing the ocean on schedule in our own day and the next time I fly across, it will be in one of them.[23]

June 25, 1932, *Boston Daily Globe*

> Everyone will use the air. For what will be called "surface flying," six hundred miles per hour will be the maximum. In the stratosphere, where there is little friction from the air and no wind, one thousand miles per hour may be expected. But stratosphere flying will be for long-distance trips, because of the time consumed in ascending and descending. The height of such flying will be more than 50,000 feet.[24]

February 1933, *Cosmopolitan*

> Weather, by [2033], will have ceased to hold a whip hand over aviation. Planes will be guided, perhaps quite automatically, through fair and foul weather by radio beacons and electrical devices from one port to another. I believe the hazards of tomorrow's flying will be fewer than those prevailing in land travel today.[25]

February 1933, *Cosmopolitan*

> In fact, it looks as if airplanes will pretty well cover the earth.[26]

Circa 1933

Cities, as we know them, will disappear. Where we commute twenty miles now, such a plane will let us commute a hundred.[27]

Circa 1934–1935

The picture, as I see it, is one of perfectly controlled transportation. Flights through the stratosphere, bringing nations to the physical status of neighbors—a network of roads built for the low, fast stream-lined cars, bringing about a daily exodus from all cities into the country—trains meeting busses—ships—meeting planes. This system shall not be confined to our nation—it is a necessary world development—it is international transportation.[29]

February 14, 1935, *Akron (OH) Beacon*

I think we may safely anticipate that there will be floating airdromes [airports] strung across the Atlantic when [transatlantic] service is started.[30]

March 7, 1935, *Boston Daily Globe*

And the day is coming when we can fold up the wings of our planes upon landing and taxi up the street to our garages.[31]

January 16, 1936, *Christian Science Monitor*

Eventually it seems to me airplanes will find it easy to go around the world. Not only around the equator, but around every way.[32]

February 12, 1937, *Christian Science Monitor*

On Accidents

Figures show that the average person flying the regular air lines will live to be 128 years old before an accident reaches him, and I beg you not to wait until you are 128 before flying.[33]

Circa 1935

Earhart and an aeronautics professor named Haskins inspecting a machine used in checking airplane motor superchargers at Purdue, April 1936.
Courtesy Purdue University Libraries, Archives and Special Collections.

4.
On Machines and Transportation

As a child, Earhart was interested in how things worked, and at age seven she designed her own roller coaster.[*] Years later, she began to pursue an engineering degree at Columbia, but she could not afford to continue after failing to secure a scholarship.[†] After she bought her first automobile, a yellow Kissel nicknamed the Yellow Peril, Earhart took an auto mechanics repair course at Smith College.[‡] Later, when she began flying, she educated herself in her planes' mechanics. As her comments indicate, Earhart believed the nation's future in machines and technology was limitless.

On Machines and Technology

How marvellous is a machine and the mind that made it. I am thoroughly occidental in this worship.[1]

Circa 1928

---

[*] Rich, 8.
[†] Winters, 49.
[‡] Van Pelt, 51; Ware, 36.

Even a new discovery is just fitting in, in the jig-saw puzzle of scientific achievement, an unusually large piece. Many little curley-kews are needed around it to make its meaning clear.[2] All kinds of minds in all kinds of schools and laboratories, or alone in cubby-holes, are trying to work out theoretical details of efficient flight. Helping them are those who put the theories to practical use.[3]

Circa 1933

Women have always had more endurance than men but they have lacked power to their blow. But now in this machine age, with the machine to help them, woman can equal, if not better, man's performances.[4]

Circa 1935

Two good engines, beautifully tuned, can sound very pretty, you know.[5]

February 12, 1937, *Christian Science Monitor*

Engines have human attributes—they usually respond to kindly treatment.[6]

March 19, 1937, *Boston Daily Globe*

I admit that women have the physical—I would rather say "reservation" than "handicap"—of not being able to strike a blow as hard as a man. But there again the machine comes to the rescue of women. With the machine age releasing her latent potentialities, a woman with a fundamental bent properly trained is equal of a man.[7]

Date unknown

On Automobiles

Those who fly owe much to those who have pioneered and developed the automobile. My own first A-B-C knowledge of gas engines was learned by working over automobile motors.[8]

July 22, 1932, *Detroit Free Press*

There is no doubt that [automobiles] are money eaters no matter how economically one tries to operate them.[9]

September 18, 1932; letter to her mother

There are of course, a great many persons driving automobiles who should not be allowed to do so. They should be given tests and the unfit ones taken off the road.[10]

March 7, 1935; Boston newspaper. At the time, drivers weren't licensed.

The automobile alone has extended a mother's responsibilities toward her children miles from home.[11]

Date unknown

On Transportation

Travel by train is a terrible waste of time. Why take six hours for a trip that can be made in one hour and 40 minutes by plane? . . . But why waste the precious daylight hours in a pokey express train?[12]

November 14, 1928, *Boston Herald*

If this prophesy [of greater airplane use] is fulfilled, railroads take warning! Put wings on your box-cars or buy a controlling interest in the right air-line.[13]

Circa 1933

Rugged individualism—the ultra-conservative and his influence—politics; these are some of the obstacles [that hold back transportation].[14]

February 14, 1935, *Akron (OH) Beacon*

Riding trains or motor cars is simply a waste of time.[15]

February 18, 1935, *Kansas City (KS) Journal*

I don't see the end of any one form of transportation but there should be more coordination of their efforts.[16]

March 30, 1935, *Minneapolis Star*

The Future of Transportation

Imagine a terminal in 2033. All forms of transportation will be part of it. From the center of a shipping area freight and passengers will be dispatched by the means which suits each best. Trains, trucks, busses, underground cars—all leave having their different burdens for different destinations over different routes. Aircraft are reached directly or at a short distance (in time) by one of the cooperating systems.[17]

February 1933, *Hearst's International-Cosmopolitan*

For the automobile of tomorrow will be streamlined as efficiently as is the airplane. The ultimate practical speeds will be regulated not by its own prowess, but by the roads provided for its use and by traffic exigencies. It may be shaped like a pear or a raindrop. Engines probably will be in the rear, eliminating sounds, odors and vibrations from the body.[18]

February 1933, *Hearst's International-Cosmopolitan*

[By 2033] systems of one-way non-intersecting highways will exist the country over. Certain of these will be exclusively for freight-carrying vehicles. On the passenger routes, speeds of one hundred miles an hour will be maintained.[19]

February 1933, *Hearst's International-Cosmopolitan*

The fundamental shift in transportation from the beginning has been one of increasing speed. This curve will continue to ascend until halted by natural laws coupled with economic expediency.[20]

February 1933, *Hearst's International-Cosmopolitan*

Earhart disembarking from her plane
at Purdue University Airport, circa 1936.
Courtesy Purdue University Libraries, Archives and Special Collections.

5.
On Business and Money

Even after her first transatlantic flight, Earhart understood that if she didn't promote herself, she wouldn't be able to keep flying. George Palmer Putnam, her manager and later husband, arranged book deals and grueling touring schedules. In 1935 she spoke to 136 groups totaling about eighty thousand people.[*] These talks funded her record-breaking flights, which in turn created more interest in her talks, which then funded more flights.

Earhart's childhood was marked by financial instability. Her father, an alcoholic, was fiscally irresponsible. Her mother, a woman of her generation who didn't work outside the home, had no control of the situation. The adult Earhart managed her own finances and kept them separate from her husband's. Putnam explained, "She recognized the value of money. She had a

---

[*] Butler, 305.

true sense of its intelligent use. But she never seemed remotely interested in accumulating wealth."*

Part of this lack of interest in money for money's sake was a result of Earhart's work with immigrants at the Denison Settlement House in Boston. Between that and traveling around the country giving speeches, Earhart saw firsthand the hardships of ordinary people.

As she became more successful, Earhart was able to send her mother a monthly allowance. She also gave money and gifts to her sister, Muriel Earhart Morrissey (nicknamed Pidge), and her family. As the years passed, however, Earhart began to resent the Morrisseys' increasing financial dependence on her.

On Business

The psychology of inferring that flying the Atlantic equips one for an advertising managership or banking, leaves me puzzled.[1]

Circa 1928. After flying the Atlantic, Earhart was presented with numerous business opportunities.

The business world will draw out one's aptitudes.[2]

Circa 1930–1937

No business is all fun. We must choose what we want to do, and we have to put in a lot of hard work to get any happiness out of it.[3]

February 19, 1935, Omaha newspaper

---

* Putnam, *Soaring Wings*, 189.

On Money and Economics

If I don't get there, I won't need it. And if I do, it will be all right.[4]

June 20, 1928, *New York Sun*; on her refusal to carry money on her 1928 transatlantic flight

I doubt whether any transatlantic flight, except one, has ever brought the personnel any net profit.[5]

August 1932, *American Magazine*. Earhart was likely referring to Lindbergh's flight.

For the woman to pay her own way may add immeasurably to the happiness of those concerned. The individual independence of dollars and cents tends to keep a healthy balance of power in the kingdom of the home.[6]

September 1932, *Redbook*

Too much relief has been aimed to help men with the theory that the men will provide for the women.[7]

December 1932, Cleveland newspaper; on federal Depression relief programs

The right to earn a living belongs to all persons. Simply to transfer the evils of poverty and overwork from one group of human beings to another is mock humanitarianism.[8]

March 7, 1933; editorial letter by Earhart supporting a minimum wage law, with equal wages for men and women

No pay, no fly, and no work, no play.[9]

Circa 1933

It's a routine now. I make a record and then I lecture on it. That's where the money comes from. Until it's time to make another record.[10]

Circa 1933

I think that every woman should earn her own living.[11]

January 12, 1934, *Columbus (OH) Citizen*

In my opinion, men and women should share financial responsibility. I think both the husband and the wife should contribute to the upkeep of the home.[12]

March 30, 1935, *Minneapolis Journal*

No economic setup of the future will be successful which does not admit women to full membership.[13]

May 2, 1935, *Boston Daily Globe*

Flying with me is a business. Of course I make money. I have to or I couldn't fly. I've got to be self-supporting or I couldn't stay in business.[14]

May 9, 1935, *New York World Telegram*

The most important subject today is modern economics. Not merely supply and demand. Demand should be what the people need. I am referring to social economics.[15]

April 7, 1936, *Post Dispatch* (St. Louis)

The economic structure we have built up is all too often a barrier between the world's work and the workers. If the younger generation finds the hurdle too absurdly high, I hope it will not hesitate to tear it down and substitute a social order in which the desire to work and earn carries with it the opportunities to do so.[16]

Unknown date

On Money Sent to Relatives

Please throw away rags and get things you need on my account at Filenes. I'll instruct them. I can do it now, and the pleasure is mine.[17]

August 26, 1928; letter to her mother, inviting her to purchase clothes at a Boston department store

I suppose it is impossible to impress upon [Muriel] the fact that [a] businesslike relationship between relatives is not an unfriendly act.... I am no Scrooge to ask that some acknowledgement of a twenty-five hundred dollar loan [be] given me. I work hard for my money. Whether or not I shall exact repayment is my business, nevertheless Pidge should feel some responsibility for protecting me against the loss of that sum.[18]

Circa April 1931; letter to her mother regarding a house loan for her sister

I am very much displeased at the use you have put [the money sent] to what I hoped you would save. I am not working to help Albert, nor Pidge much as I care for her. If they had not had that money perhaps they would have found means to economize before. I do not mean to be harsh, but I know the family failing about money.[19]

Circa autumn 1931; letter to her mother. Earhart resented her brother-in-law and sister for squandering money.

Enclosed is a check. Please don't give it all away if the giving means fostering dependence and lack of responsibility.[20]

February 13, 1933; letter to her mother

Please remember you and Pidge attract attention as my relatives so spare me blowsies.[*] I'd prefer you to get a few simple decent clothes, both of you. Not awful cheepies, so people who don't look below the surface won't have anything to converse about.[21]

July 5, 1935; letter to her mother

On Poverty

Why should I have so much—even just this car—and that man so little? I don't know the answer. But there is one. There *must* be. You can't say I've aspired to do something with whatever capacities I have, and that such a man hasn't—but that can't be the answer. It *can't* be.[22]

Date unknown; reaction to seeing an elderly homeless man

---

[*] being sloppy and unkempt

Earhart in the cockpit, circa 1937.
Courtesy Library of Congress Prints and Photographs Division.

6.
On Work

Earhart's mother kept a shared baby book for her two daughters. Muriel's birth on a Friday was recorded with the adage "Friday's bairn is loving and giving." Amelia was born on a Saturday, and her adage reads, "But Saturday's bairn must work for his living."[*] The maxim was prophetic in Earhart's case. She turned out to be a tireless worker.

In 1932 the aviatrix claimed, "I've had twenty-eight different jobs in my life, and I hope I'll have 288 more."[†] Among other things, she was an assistant nurse, a telephone company clerk, a social worker, a promoter of airlines, and of course a pilot. She also started her own clothing line and served as a career consultant for women at Purdue University.[‡]

Earhart felt that thanks to the Industrial Revolution, machines

---

[*] Earhart baby book, "Baby's Kingdom," SLRC, A-129, series II, 7.
[†] Earhart, "Flying the Atlantic—and Selling Sausages Have a Lot of Things in Common," *American Magazine*, August 1932, 72.
[‡] Butler, 300–303; Lovell, 220, 222–26.

had rendered the drudgery of traditional "women's work" obsolete (See chapter 4, "On Machines and Transportation"). As a result, she believed the professions should be open to women on an equal footing with men. Though she acknowledged that it might take time for women to achieve parity, she discouraged protective legislation (see chapter 5, "On Business and Money," and chapter 7, "On Politics and Government") for female workers. Women, she believed, could stand on their own two feet.

On Work

There must be a sincere interest in the work, a love for it, and a hunger and a longing for it, just as there must be in a nurse before she gives herself over to that work, or an actress, or a surgeon, or a teacher—or a wife. Of course, not everyone can find just the right work, but those who can are fortunate; there is nothing more satisfying.[1]

October 1933, *Independent Woman*

It doesn't matter at all what one does after leaving college, for the business world will bring out one's aptitudes.[2]

May 17, 1936, *Ogden (UT) Standard-Examiner*

Fun is the indispensable part of work.[3]

Date unknown

Such people must know they're in the right profession. The rest of us, I fear, can never know for certain until we can take a backward look in old age, for we must have a background of experience against which to make comparisons.[4]

Date unknown

Of course, if men and women are very unhappy in their work, they are entitled to a pretty good opinion that they are in the wrong work. Yet if they are happy in it—I don't believe it means, necessarily, that they couldn't be happier.[5]

Date unknown

If you want to try a certain job, try it. Then if you find something on the morrow that looks better, make a change.[6]

Date unknown

On Social Work

Rewards are gain in knowledge; personal satisfaction in accomplishing what must be done in untangling human complexities; and a feeling that the ultimate reason for life is that it can be a beautiful thing, and that I, as well as others, will reap the reward of that. Drawbacks are lack of time for much beauty in life—time for study, time for people, time for physical exercise. . . . Lack of all these partly due to inadequate pay.[7]

Circa 1927–1928

To me one of the biggest jobs of the social worker is to give boys and girls the experiences that will keep them young.[8]

Date unknown

Social work does not begin and end with philanthropy, though that is an important phase of it. Social work to me is essentially education, for it is synonymous with the ability to make adjustments to poverty, illness, illiteracy and any other morbid conditions; and in order to make such an adjustment competently, the first requisite is a sound education. Social services should be preventive rather than curative.[9]

Date unknown

But I *still* do social service—by lecturing, writing, speaking over the radio. It may be a different kind of social service from that of a Settlement. But after all, my social work there had been more than the mere teaching of the correct use of English words.[10]

Date unknown; Earhart's reaction to criticism for leaving social work

On Women in Work and Careers

The woman who can create her own job is the woman who will win fame and fortune.[11]

Circa 1928

I think a special cheer should go out to the married ones who have gone right ahead even though their husbands were not interested or were even downright discouraging.[12]

July 26, 1931, *San Diego Union*

Women who might make good mechanics are shunted into cooking.[13]

July 1931, *Golden Book Magazine*

The time is not far distant when women will have equal chance with men in working out a career.[14]

September 25, 1932, *Richmond (VA) Times Dispatch*

It is fortunately no longer a disgrace to be undomestic, and married women should be able to seek, as unrestrictedly as men, any gainful occupation their talents and interests make available.[15]

September 1932, *Redbook*

It isn't news to us that our presence is often undesired, so we're especially alert to our shortcomings—poor relatives in the houses of the mighty. However, we have enough intelligence to subject the mighty to the same scrutiny which we turn upon ourselves—bold hussies that we are.[16]

Circa 1932

Women can do most things men can do.... To say that women can do anything that men can do is absurd. What I contend is that women, in any job that requires intelligence, coordination, spirit, coolness, and will power (without too heavy muscular strength) are able to meet men on their own ground.[17]

August 1932, *American Magazine*

Welcome us into industry, pay us fairly, treat us as economic beings with wills of our own. Women in the home weren't parasites—and we aren't going to begin a parasitical existence now![18]

June 3, 1934, *Plain Dealer* (Cleveland, OH)

[A woman's] place is wherever her individual aptitude places her. There is no such thing as men's work or women's work.[19]

March 30, 1935, *Minneapolis Star*

Women should strive for goals outside of what is known as their "sphere." Women must learn to do for themselves what men have done for themselves. I long for the day when individual aptitude, regardless of sex, will be the criterion by which a person is judged.[20]

March 31, 1935, *Los Angeles Times*

When you graduate be sure you go on and have a career; don't get married as soon as you get out of school.[21]

Circa 1935–1937; advice to female Purdue University students

I believe that a girl should not do what she thinks she should do, but should find out through experience what she wants to do.[22]

May 17, 1936, *Seattle Daily Times*

It is just as important to give work to women as men, for they have an equal need for mental stimulus and feeling of accomplishment and economic independence.[23]

May 17, 1936, *Seattle Daily Times*

If women are eventually found in locomotive cabs, building bridges, or chasing bandits as normal occupations, it will be no surprise to me.[24]

Date unknown

Millions of women are earning their living. Some because they have to, some because they want to. But none of it would be possible if science and invention hadn't basically altered the industrial system.[25]

Date unknown

When women are really able to take the long view of economics, they will abandon their sentimental attitude about protective legislation for women, minimum hours and minimum wages for women. Limited wages and hours are only protecting the infantile period of women and work to the disadvantage of those who want to progress. Wages should be based on work itself, not on sex or any other consideration.[26]

Date unknown

And it does seem to me that if a woman can earn more at the same job than she can save by working at home, she should not be hampered in taking the job. If her husband didn't happen to have more lucrative work at hand, why shouldn't he take over the home job, and with no sense of hurt pride? I realize, of course, that the whole concept will encounter storms of good horselaughs—but even that doesn't seem to me to invalidate it as a working idea.[27]

Date unknown

On Women Working in the Home and Housework

It seems to me two hours a day should be sufficient. And where there are children, possibly a good deal of the time given to them might be divided between husbands and wives, especially if the wives do some of the earning.[28]

February 6, 1932, *Times-Picayune* (New Orleans, LA)

Even if one holds that a woman's whole interest should be in her home, it must be remembered that the home is no longer confined between four walls as it was in past generations. Modern transportation has extended the home beyond such narrow confines—and women must extend their spheres if they are to help their children cope with their problems.[29]

February 4, 1933, *Seattle Post-Intelligencer*

Women are changing. I think the woman who spends all her time in managing a household must be stupid. I spend at least half my time at home—Three servants, a secretary. It's not a large household, but it does take a little management and I find I can do it without difficulty.[30]

November 23, 1933, *Journal American* (New York, NY)

It has been in the home that the application of scientific discovery have been most far-reaching. For science has released women from so much of the age-old drudgery connected with the mere process of living.[31]

Date unknown

For the first time in history women are being permitted to think outside the home, and I believe that actually emphasis on homemaking is almost the least necessity of their development. They have been so close to the whole idea of homemaking that they are almost wholly without perspective. At the same time, the men have been indirectly taught to regard homemaking problems as being entirely outside their province. Where homemaking is given as a college course, the implication is always that running the house is automatically a career, and, as such, justifies a wife accepting food, shelter, clothing, etc., from her husband. It seems to me such reasoning is very faulty when one considers the difference between the work women did a hundred years ago and what is necessary today.[32]

Date unknown

On Rest and Retirement

Not while there's life left in the old horse.[33]

January 13, 1935, *Boston Daily Globe*; response to a question about retiring from long-distance flying

Every once in a while you have to pull yourself up and stop doing things. You can't rush around doing things all the time. It's good to stop and look around and find out what the whole thing means.[34]

August 25, 1935, *Dayton Daily News*

I dream that by working very hard I'll have some time later to watch sunsets. If I cannot earn peace by activity, I think I'll take time anyway before I grow unappreciative of beauty.[35]

Date unknown

President Herbert Hoover and Earhart at the White House, 1932.
Courtesy Library of Congress Prints and Photographs Division.

7.
On Politics and Government

Amelia Earhart never spoke publicly about her political leanings, but not because of the era's long-standing proscription against women's involvement in the messy, masculine business of politics. Earhart had no problem resisting conventional roles and speaking her mind. Instead, her reluctance was more likely a wish to stay on good terms with those who could keep her in the air.

Earhart understood the importance of remaining nonpartisan in a nation polarized between those who supported Franklin Roosevelt's New Deal policies and his opposition, which viewed the administration as a hair's breadth away from socialism. Earhart admired First Lady Eleanor Roosevelt but had doubts about her husband.

In 1933, at her insistence, President Roosevelt appointed her friend Eugene Vidal to the position of director of the Bureau of Air Commerce. Three years later, when reorganization threatened Vidal's job, Earhart refused to support the president unless he was reinstated. It was an election year. Vidal kept his job.

Governmental assistance was essential for Earhart's round-the-world trip. She required permission to land in foreign countries, visas, logistical aid, and access to reliable fuel supplies. On November 10, 1936, she wrote a confidential letter to President Roosevelt requesting his help.[*] He laughed at her daring and ordered his administration, "Do what you can."[†] Government-funded advisers, facilities, and resources were placed at her disposal. Roosevelt's Works Progress Administration even built a runway on Howland Island for Earhart.[‡]

On Government, Politics, and Policies

So far as I can see, humanity must develop through restriction of liberty until able to understand freedom.[1]

Circa 1930; on the subject of Prohibition

But after all, Messieurs, it is far more difficult and important to make good laws than it is to fly the Atlantic.[2]

June 7, 1932; speech to the French senate. The president responded, "Ah, Madame, when you fly the ocean, what you do is a danger only to yourself, while the laws we make are a danger to so many!"

Subsidies should be best directed toward providing essential aids that no private business would be justified in providing for itself.[3]

March 16, 1934, *Christian Science Monitor*

---

[*] Letter from Earhart to Franklin Delano Roosevelt, November 10, 1937, Franklin D. Roosevelt Presidential Library and Museum, Hyde Park, NY; hereafter FDRL.
[†] Butler, 350.
[‡] Winters, 177–81.

Frankly, I believe the present administration has recognized the rights of women far more than ever did its predecessors, despite the depression, which too often has created legislation unjust to working women.[4]

Circa 1934–1935; on the Roosevelt administration

The forces of evolution are so much stronger than "deals" or political parties, that human and scientific developments will ultimately triumph over inadequate systems of government.[5]

February 14, 1935, *Akron (OH) Beacon*; referring to Roosevelt's New Deal

Please don't down the Roosevelt administration. It's all right to be reactionary inside but it is out of step with the times to sound off about the chosen people who have inherited or grabbed the earth. You must think of me when you converse and I believe the experiments carried out today point the way to a new social order when governments will be the voice of the proletariat far more than a democracy ever can be.[6]

Circa spring 1936; letter to her mother

There is little use of my trying to interest others in the President's cause when my heart is sick with the knowledge that an industry can be jeopardized and an individual's career blasted by what seems a personal feud.[7]

September 15, 1936; telegram from Earhart to Eleanor Roosevelt, threatening to withdraw support for the president if Eugene Vidal was not reinstated

I am aligned with President Roosevelt because of his social conscience. Throughout his term of office he has fought against odds to reduce human misery. He has realized that obsolescence can affect parts of the machinery of government just as it does the machinery of industry.[8]

September 20, 1936, *New York Times*

On Government Pensions

I think the government ought to make people save some of their wages and give it back to them when they are old. . . . I think we should have had the right to talk it out tonight instead of being sent home like naughty children.[9]

Circa 1920. As a young woman, Earhart attended a meeting of the Industrial Workers of the World, a socialist group. The meeting was broken up by police. President Roosevelt signed the Social Security Act in 1935.

On Laws

Until a better race is bred, I fear prohibitory laws, such as those against murder, theft, etc., will have to be in force. Ultimately, all can be modified, when civilization knows how to prevent anti-social acts rather than being forced to punish after their commission.[10]

Date unknown

Earhart in her volunteer nurse uniform, circa 1917–1918.
Courtesy Schlesinger Library, Radcliffe Institute, Harvard University.

8.
On War

In December 1917, when the nation was embroiled in World War I, Earhart was not satisfied knitting sweaters for the troops with her finishing school classmates. While visiting her sister Muriel in Toronto, Earhart dropped out of school and became a nurse with Canada's Voluntary Aid Detachment.[*] Comforting and caring for men riddled with gunshot wounds, missing limbs, and suffering from mustard gas poisoning and shell shock turned her into a fervent pacifist.

Earhart was vocal in her opposition to militarism. In 1933, in an address to the Daughters of the American Revolution, she drew gasps when she criticized the organization's support for military preparedness.[†] Even more controversial, she advanced the then-scandalous notion that women should be drafted as well as men.

---

[*] Butler, 82; Ware, 34.
[†] "Woman Flier Scolds DAR," *Springfield (MA) Republican*, April 22, 1933.

On War

Four men on crutches, walking together on King Street in Toronto that winter, was a sight which changed the course of existence for me. The realization that war wasn't knitting sweaters and selling Liberty Bonds, nor dancing with handsome uniforms was suddenly evident.[1]

Circa 1928; regarding her experiences in 1917

There for the first time I realized what the World War meant. Instead of new uniforms and brass bands, I saw only the result of a four years' desperate struggle; men without arms and legs, men who were paralyzed and men who were blind.[2]

Circa 1928; regarding her experiences in 1917

There is so much that must be done in a civilized barbarism like war.[3]

Circa 1928

It is fair to suppose that in any wars which the future may bring, aviation will figure as never before.[4]

March 1929, *Hearst's International-Cosmopolitan*

I feel that war must end or what we now call civilization will be ended.[5]

February 2, 1933, *Morning Oregonian* (Portland)

Women could work behind the lines bringing up supplies. They could be made pilots for observation planes and other types of ships if the generals don't want us to fly fighting craft. Do you know women may be even more desperate flyers than men, we've never been tried out. I think the women should be drafted for fighting service in the next war along with the men. I think it would be the finest possible way to end war.[6]

February 2, 1933, *Morning Oregonian* (Portland)

I am entirely against war, but the fact that women were drafted for service might be a means of stopping it. To some it is easier to go to war than to say no. Real knowledge of war might help women oppose it.[7]

February 4, 1933, *Vancouver Daily Province*

Possibly, if women had knowledge of actual combat, it would put an entirely different face on war. Many men go to war now as if it were . . . a junket. Women would eliminate that.[8]

February 5, 1933, unnamed Los Angeles newspaper

We glorify war now, using all sorts of propaganda to make it more colorful. If women went to war, had actual combat, it might shock civilization into a realization of the waste and tragedy.[9]

February 5, 1933, unnamed Los Angeles newspaper

How many men would go to war, if they knew their wives might be drafted the next day? Women have learned that sacrifice.[10]

February 5, 1933, unnamed Los Angeles newspaper

I feel that no organization should advocate armaments unless they themselves are willing to bear arms also.[11]

April 21, 1933, address to the Daughters of the American Revolution

As an individual I'm opposed to war and naturally I think it is extremely unfortunate that war should be emphasized, and to some extent glorified, in any kind of film. . . . the destructive possibilities of aviation are its least important attribute and . . . to put chief emphasis on the airplane as a weapon of war would be to distort its true place in the scheme of things.[12]

June 1933, *Screenland*

Also I believe the oldest people should be drafted first. They are the ones who start war, and if they knew that their verdict to fight meant their getting out in the line of fire themselves, they would be a great deal slower in rushing into an armed conflict.[13]

November 11, 1933, *New York Times*

I cannot understand how civilized people can want war. But, if there must be war, women should share its responsibilities equally with men.[14]

Circa 1933–1934

I am particularly distressed at the unfair use of my name by one who seems to be a professional arms lobbyist and salesman, for I am whole-heartedly aligned against war and the makers thereof.[15]

September 11, 1934, *Evening Tribune* (San Diego, CA). Earhart was incensed to find that a munitions dealer claimed to have her support.

We are citizens, paying taxes—which are too largely spent for armaments. So why should we not participate in a military system we help support? . . . To kill, to suffer, to be maimed, wasted, paralyzed, impoverished, to lose mental and physical vigor, to shovel under the dead, to die oneself—"gloriously." There is no logic in disqualifying women from such privileges.[16]

August 1935, *Home Magazine*

Aviation was the romantic branch of the service. No one looked beyond the swank uniforms to the picture of airplanes crippled in mid-air, carrying their occupants earthward, helplessly, hopelessly.[17]

August 1935, *Home Magazine*; referring to aviation during World War I

If women go to war, along with their men, the men are just going to hate it! If they hate it enough, perhaps they will give up wars altogether. And that would be one of the many useful accomplishments of women's emergence as "persons."[18]

August 1935, *The Home Magazine*

I revolt against the senselessness of all wars.[19]

August 1935, *The Home Magazine*

Youth can escape the dark implications of war because it never projects itself into the disagreeable situations, but thinks only in terms of nebulous others who are doomed to die.[20]

August 1935, *The Home Magazine*

The Crusades would have been much less fun than the Crusaders found them if women had tagged along.[21]

Unknown date

> Of course, once we got a serious discussion of such a draft [of women], we should hear Chivalry crying to Heaven that females are much too frail to be subjected to the inhuman cruelties and hardships of what is, after all, "a man's game." Nonsense![22]
>
> Unknown date

Earhart visiting a class in the Department of Botany and Plant Pathology at Purdue, circa 1935–1937.
Courtesy Purdue University Libraries, Archives and Special Collections.

9.
On Education

Earhart's education was inconsistent. She was homeschooled and attended both public and private schools due to her family's precarious financial circumstances and frequent relocations. Despite this, Earhart excelled academically. Her 1919 report card lists top marks in French, German, economics, geometry, composition, accounting, psychology, spelling, Bible studies, art, current events, and exercise but only fair marks in punctuality and tidiness.[*]

In 1919 Earhart entered the premed program at Columbia University. After a year, she decided she wasn't cut out to become a doctor. Later she considered engineering, but she couldn't afford to stay in school.[†] Though her formal education ended when she withdrew from Columbia, Earhart continued to educate herself throughout her life.

---

[*] Morrissey and Osborne, 45.
[†] Butler, 118–19.

On Education

Of course I'm going to B.M. [Bryn Mawr] if I have to drive a grocery wagon to accumulate the cash.[1]

March 7, 1914; letter to Virginia Park. Earhart did not attend Bryn Mawr.

Girls have had fewer opportunities to express their mechanical bent. Yet some of them would prove better carpenters than cooks, just as some boys would make better pies than machines.[2]

May 26, 1929, *New York Times*

I remember teaching a class of boys cooking, and they were just as backward at their cooking lessons as woman is over mechanics.[3]

July 15, 1930, *Seattle Daily Times*

The education system is based on sex, not on aptitude.[4]

May 9, 1931, *New York Times*

Experiment! Meet new people. Find out about them. Adapt yourself to them, please them, anger them, study them! That's better than any college education. *You will find the unexpected everywhere as you go through life.* By adventuring about you become accustomed to the unexpected. The unexpected then becomes what it really is—the inevitable. But you are ready for it—flexible, realistic, tolerant, hard-boiled, and sympathetic.[5]

August 1932, *American Magazine*

Everything I have studied that I was interested in has given me something.[6]

Circa 1933

Too often little attention is paid to individual talent. Instead, education goes on dividing people according to their sex, and putting them in little feminine or masculine pigeonholes.[7]

Circa 1933

I think you children should be exposed to every possible kind of learning. I think you should be able to discover for yourselves the jobs you want to do.[8]

Circa 1933; speech to children at the Institute of Arts in Detroit

Educators, in general, need to be more practical in their instruction. Too much emphasis is placed on learning a skill without finding out whether the student has a natural bent or talent for that particular work or whether the business or industrial world needs that person where he or she is trained.[9]

Circa 1934–1935

Purdue is my type of school. It is a technical school, where instruction has practicality and where a progressive program for women was started.[10]

Circa 1934–1935

Universities and colleges have gone blindly on producing hundreds of graduates who demand jobs of a world for which they, despite their formal education, may be totally unprepared or unfitted.[11]

November 27, 1935, *Indianapolis News*

Yet today it is true that there is little or nothing in the educational setup to instill very real and vital desires. There never has been the synchronization between academic training and the economic world that there could and should be.[12]

November 27, 1935, Indianapolis News

I feel that education fails to discover individual aptitudes soon enough. I hope that the time will come soon when psychologists and psychiatrists will be able to determine a child's bent in the pre-school age, then he won't waste so much time studying and working at the wrong things.[13]

May 17, 1936, Seattle Daily Times

Experience seems to be the most potent determining factor in choice of careers, and boys and girls can't acquire that until college is over.[14]

May 17, 1936, Seattle Daily Times

Many a stay-at-home girl would welcome practical training in what to do when the door-bell fails to function, the plumbing clogs, the gas-range leaks, the fuse blows out, the windmill pump goes haywire, and the thousand-and-one other mechanical indispositions that can occur around the house, often easily fixed if one has rudimentary knowledge of how to fix them.[15]

Circa 1937

On Writing

My book goes to press very soon. I should like to have made it better but time was short and I done as good as I could.[16]

Circa 1928

Frankly, I'm far from confident of its air-worthiness, and don't know how to rate its literary horse-power or estimate its cruising radius and climbing ability. Confidentially, it may never even make the take-off. If the crash comes, at least there'll be no fatalities. No one can see more comedy in the disaster than the author herself. Especially because even the writing of the book, like so much else of the flight and its aftermaths, has had its humor—some of it publishable.[17]

Circa 1928; on *20 Hrs., 40 Min.*

Today, if you ever figure in any unusual exploit, be it a flight, a voyage in a small boat, or, say, a channel swim, paraphrasing Alice in Wonderland, "There's a publisher close behind you who is treading on your heels." Writing a book seems inevitable.[18]

Circa 1932

On Reading and Books

Books have meant much to me. Not only did I myself read considerably, but Mother read aloud to my sister and me, early and later. So fundamental became the habit that on the occasions when we girls had to do housework, instead of both pitching in and doing it together, one was selected to read aloud and the other to work.[19]

Circa 1932

Perhaps the fact that I was exceedingly fond of reading made me endurable.[20]

Circa 1933; on her childhood reading habits

> It is unfortunate but not surprising that aviation has not produced anything [literary] of real beauty yet. There are adequate descriptions of the process of flying and its technicalities. . . . Aviation fiction runs the gamut from the cheapest thrills to pretty fair products. However there seems to be none that one could really hug close and cherish.[21]
>
> Date unknown

> No one can scan the shelves of teen-age reading matter without being struck with the fact that girls are evidently not expected to join in the fun. There are no heroines following the shining paths of romantic adventure, as do the heroes of boys' books. . . . No, goings-on of this sort are left to masculine characters, to be lived over joyously by the boy readers. . . . Instead of closing the covers with shining eyes and the happy thought, "That might happen to me someday!" the girl, turning the final page, can only sigh regretfully, "Oh, dear, that can never happen to me—because I'm not a boy.[22]
>
> Date unknown

Earhart sitting on top of her Lockheed Electra with Purdue students,
September 20, 1936.
Courtesy Purdue University Libraries, Archives and Special Collections.

10.
On Gender and Age

Most strong women who stepped outside traditional gender roles, especially those who encouraged others to do the same, were roundly criticized by society. Not Earhart. Politicians, the press, and the public praised her. In aviation circles, she was almost universally admired by male and female pilots.

Perhaps part of this acceptance was due to Earhart's modest and self-deprecating sense of humor. She was quick to credit others for their accomplishments. Additionally, she didn't fit the image of a radical feminist. She was tall, slim, and quiet. Her tousled hair and freckles gave her a girl-next-door persona. Even a reporter who found everything else about her reprehensible declared Earhart "delightfully feminine."[*]

Nonetheless, Earhart's message was controversial. A member of the National Women's Party, she believed women deserved the

---

[*] "Amelia Earhart Flies to the Defense of Her Sex as a 'Disgusted Male' Cries: Women are a Total Flop outside the Home," *Plain Dealer* (Cleveland, OH), June 3, 1934.

same educational (see chapter 9, "On Education") and professional (see chapter 6, "On Work") opportunities as men.* She praised women who stepped out of traditional roles. Even more controversial, she believed that husbands should have the same child-rearing responsibilities as wives.

Many seem to have been so charmed by Earhart that they missed her message, but not all. A 1932 editorial in the *New York World Telegram* credited Earhart with marshaling in a new era: "[Thanks to Earhart,] men have no monopoly on daring nowadays, and modern women, delighting in their freedom, have several thousand years of adventureless security to make up for!"† Earhart was proud to be the standard bearer for a new generation.

On Gender

And the nicest thing that has happened to me is having all these men stand and sing "For She's a Jolly Good Fellow."[1]

May 24, 1932, *Boston Daily Globe*. Following her solo transatlantic flight, British pilots sang in her honor.

A woman may even one day be President of the United States.[2]

September 25, 1932, *Richmond (VA) Times Dispatch*

It's time biology and sex were squeezed out of accomplishment and we were all looked at as persons.[3]

December 12, 1932, *Toronto Daily Star*

---

* Lovell, 196; Ware, 123–27.
† Gretta Palmer, "Miss Earhart's Feat Hints New Exploits by Fearless Women," *New York World Telegram*, May 23, 1932.

So far as sex is concerned, women are no more valuable than men. It's the individual's personal worth that counts.[4]

February 4, 1933, *Vancouver (BC) Daily Province*

Sex has been used too long as a subterfuge by the inefficient woman who likes to make herself and others believe that it is not her incapability but her womanhood which is holding her back.[5]

Circa 1933

Women have to do so many things that men have done just to prove they can.[6]

February 2, 1934, *Richmond (VA) Times Dispatch*

Tradition with a capital T bars women from everything.[7]

February 2, 1934, *Richmond (VA) Times Dispatch*

In both sexes you will find good, bad and just average.[8]

June 3, 1934, *Plain Dealer* (Cleveland, OH)

I look for a bright and happy day in which individual aptitude will be a criterion, and not sex.[9]

February 23, 1935, *Morning Star* (Rockford, IL)

When it comes to mechanical ability, there isn't any sex—how could there be? It depends on the individual. There is no reason in the world why a woman should not have as complete a grasp on mechanics than a man.[10]

Circa May 1935

After all, what is sauce for the goose is also sauce for the gander and if both men and women fly, it is only serving science to investigate both for comparison.[11]

October 7, 1935; letter to Dr. Raymond S. Holtz

On Gender Roles in the Home

And then too, I believe that a man is just as responsible as a woman for the success of the home; if both are working, they should share this responsibility.[12]

January 23, 1933, *The Campus* (Sarah Lawrence College, Bronxville, NY)

Every man should be required to do some of the housework. It's no fun; it's just hard work. And the men ought to know it.[13]

January 12, 1934, *Columbus (OH) Citizen*

Women should earn their own salt and men should do their part of the housework. They should help bring up the children too![14]

February 2, 1934, *Richmond (VA) Times Dispatch*

Women should know the grind of a job, and men, the drudgery of housework. There would be fewer misunderstandings.[15]

May 18, 1934, *Springfield (MA) Republican*

No woman who has not worked for a living can possibly understand the weariness and worries of a man who slaves all day in an office. And no man who has never washed a dish, scrubbed a floor or cared for a baby can possibly understand what drudgery and nerve strain women have always undergone. When they share each other's everyday tasks, when the woman learns what it is to run a desk, and the man learns what it is to do housework, you begin to engender mutual sympathy.[16]

June 3, 1934, *Plain Dealer* (Cleveland, OH)

On Men

I loathe watching men. Why can't they be more responsible?[17]

Circa June 1928. Having a father who was an alcoholic, Earhart was uncomfortable with her male flying companions' consumption of alcohol.

Men have been "civilized" and experienced for centuries. Surely men have had plenty of time to acquire a fine finish, to get the rough edges of their conduct polished off. And yet— look at their record.[18]

June 3, 1934, *Plain Dealer* (Cleveland, OH)

Paul is flying the plane. Men seem better pleased to have a male confederate, though it is my shop Paul flies. When a principle is not at stake I let them have their way.[19]

September 1935; on Paul Mantz flying her plane

I do think American men are outstanding in their keen responsibility as providers. Now if they would only adopt the idea of getting into the kitchen once in a while too, it seems to be they would be reasonably perfect![20]

Date unknown

On Women

Women are on the defensive and must prove their mettle by doing things.[21]

July 1929, *Hearst's International-Cosmopolitan*

We hear much of women's "nerves." They may be different in some ways, but it seems to me, given a similar education, those differences would tend to disappear. A woman can sew, watch two or three things on the stove, keep an eye on three or four children, and remain unperturbed. Half an hour in a similar situation for a man completely shatters his nervous system.[22]

July 1929, *Hearst's International-Cosmopolitan*

[Women] have opened so many doors marked "Impossible" that I don't know where they'll stop.[23]

April/May 1930, *Aero News and Mechanics*

The trouble nowadays, as it has been always, woman is bred to timidity. This is what handicaps them. From the time they first go to school little girls are taught to be afraid of certain things. In reality most women are just as strong as men. In fact they could do most things as well as men if they were only educated the same way.[24]

July 15, 1930, *Seattle Daily Times*. Earhart was influenced by Dora Russell, author of *The Right to Be Happy* (1927), who described women as being bred for timidity.

The sheltered, pampered type of femininity is passé. Ignorance has ceased to be a charm.[25]

April 19, 1931, *Times-Picayune* (New Orleans, LA)

With their mother's milk little girls commence to absorb "don't and can'ts and mustn'ts." You know the stuff. Well, we aren't really a civilized people until such foolishness is stopped.[26]

December 12, 1932, *Toronto Daily Star*

To say women seek security instead of freedom is silly.[27]

December 12, 1932, *Toronto Daily Star*

I think that in 1933 more women should strive to look beyond the horizon of their homes and assume greater responsibility in political and economic fields. To do this they must seek accurate knowledge of present day problems, find courage for independent action and learn to cooperate better with one another for their own good and that of the world in general.[28]

January 1, 1933, *Aberdeen (SD) Daily News*

Without the background of knowing the full value of experience, I sometimes think women are more apt to attempt a bigger bite than they can successfully chew than are men.[29]

Circa 1933

Women must try to do things as men have tried. When they fail, their failure must be but a challenge to others.[30]

January 8, 1935; letter from Earhart to George Putnam

Women always have a burden of criticism in any undertaking.[31]

January 13, 1935, *Boston Daily Globe*

Women should do for themselves what men have already done for themselves.[32]

February 22, 1935, Indiana newspaper

Women should strive for goals outside what is platitudinously called their "sphere." ... There is no reason why women should not do anything that men can do.[33]

August 10, 1935, *Chautauqua (NY) Daily*

The woman of today is a different creature from one of the last century who dropped off so easily into a fit of the vapours.[34]

October 7, 1935; letter to Dr. Raymond S. Holtz regarding the possible effects of menstruation on a woman's job performance

As tasks tend to be allotted on the basis of individual aptitude and ability, more women will have opportunity where now they are stopped one by legislation, two by lack of training, three by traditional barriers.[35]

November 9, 1935; telegram from Earhart to Jo Berger

Women are interested industrially, economically. And I don't think it means that the maternal, the domestic instinct is erased in their attitude. The home is still predominant, but modern appliances—the machine age—have corrected things so that women have more leisure to adapt themselves to an outside sphere.[36]

December 2, 1935, *New York World Telegram*

We have almost obliterated the tradition of homes and babies.[37]

December 2, 1935, *New York World Telegram*

Because this world has been arranged heretofore so that women could not be active as individuals, it has been assumed that they neither want to nor ever could be.[38]

Date unknown

The mental attitude toward sex isn't what it was a decade ago. At that time a girl's only salvation was marriage; and mothers were terribly humiliated if their daughters didn't go off at 21. That belonged to a past when a woman's interests were centered around the kitchen and when she used to suffer the "spring-cleaning hysteria." But now that we know better and look back, we stop and wonder why it ever was that way.[39]

Unknown date

On Women as Drivers

Women drivers of cars are as careful as most men drivers and a great many of them know as much about their cars as do men. Trust woman's natural inquisitiveness to find out what is under the hood.[40]

April 19, 1931, *Times-Picayune* (New Orleans, LA)

On Discrimination against Women

Society pushes men forward and holds women back.[41]

July 30, 1929, *New York Times*

I know from practical experience of the discriminations which confront women when they enter an occupation where men have priority in opportunity, advancement and protection.[42]

September 23, 1932, *New York Times*

> In every State of the Union today there are discriminations against women in the law. I join with the National Woman's party in hoping for the speedy passage of the Lucretia Mott amendment, which would write into the highest law of our land that men and women shall have equal rights throughout the United States and every place subject to its jurisdiction.[43]

September 23, 1932, *New York Times*. Every year from 1923 to 1942, the National Woman's Party proposed an amendment to Congress, stating, "Men and women shall have equal rights throughout the United States and every place subject to its jurisdiction." It never passed.[*]

> We must get rid of discrimination against women in every line of human activity.[44]

March 16, 1934, *Christian Science Monitor*

> Chivalry must be spurious. Too often today it blandly averts its gaze from the women of the world who do so much of the dirty work, often in the face of discrimination against their sex rather than for it. Women are strong enough to scrub office buildings, stand on their feet at wash-tubs all day, and work in the fields.[45]

August 1935, *The Home Magazine*

> I've had practical experience and know the discrimination against women in various forms of industry. A pilot's a pilot. I hope that such equality could be carried out in other fields so that men and women may achieve equally in any endeavor they set out.[46]

Date unknown

---

[*] See Faulkner.

On Feminism

Doubtless by now I am running the risk of becoming a heavy handed feminist. In a measure, I'm guilty, as I do become increasingly weary of male supremacy unquestioned.[47]

September 1931, *Hearst's International-Cosmopolitan*

I cannot claim to be a feminist, but do rather enjoy seeing women tackling all kinds of new problems—new for them, that is.[48]

Date unknown

On Equal Rights

I'd like to see men's and women's records and a sexless thing called a world's record in all activities, flying being no exception.[49]

July 1929, *Hearst's International-Cosmopolitan*. Despite her desire for equality, Earhart thought that women should set records separately from men, at least until their access to training and other resources became equitable.

When women really know about economics, take a long view of the subject, they will abandon this sentimental attitude about protective legislation for women, minimum hours and minimum wages for women. Limited hours and limited pay only prolong the infantile period of women and work to the disadvantage of those who want to progress. Wages should be based on work, not sex nor any other consideration. The problem should be not minimum scales for women but minimum scales for everybody.[50]

April 7, 1936, *Post Dispatch* (St. Louis)

> I am deeply interested in women's obtaining full equality under the law. . . . Today women still stand victims of restrictive class legislation and conflicting interpretations of statues. . . . their rights must be made theirs by definition, that is by Constitutional guarantee.[51]
>
> November 15, 1936; message to the National Woman's Party convention

On Youth

> Young people and old people, too, are too timid about experimenting, trying their little adventures, flying their own Atlantics. Step out! Try the job you are interested in! Use the talents which give you joy. There's plenty of time.[52]
>
> August 1932, *American Magazine*

> All youngsters today are sold on aviation. Think what that means for its future.[53]
>
> December 1, 1934, *Minneapolis Tribune*

> The ancients, such as I am, should be listening to young ideas rather than pointing up opportunities in a world which has the elders decidedly on the run![54]
>
> Circa 1934. She was thirty-seven at the time.

> I believe that youth faces the greatest era for creative accomplishment in history. With the radio, aviation, and transportation only partially developed, and international understanding and peace still a hope, every road is open. If these girls and boys

will leave behind them the influence of this material age, and create for the love of accomplishment and its importance in building a new social order, they will not need the sympathy now extended to them.[55]

February 14, 1935, *Akron (OH) Beacon*

Don't be reactionary with Nancy. Let her be radical. Youth which isn't is pretty poor and all her family are sticks.[56]

Circa spring 1936; letter to her mother about relations with a relative

On Elders

Some elders have to be shocked for everybody's good now and then. Doing so, sometimes is a little hard on the shockers, however.[57]

Circa 1933

Earhart and her husband, George Palmer Putnam,
at the Purdue Airport, circa 1935–1937.
Courtesy Purdue University Libraries, Archives and Special Collections.

11.
On Marriage, Parenting, and Birth Control

Earhart's parents' marriage was unhappy. Edwin Earhart, a railroad claims agent, never became the successful inventor or lawyer he envisioned himself to be. As he descended into unemployment and alcoholism, his wife, Amy Otis Earhart, became resentful and controlling. Earhart's parents divorced in 1924.[*]

Prior to her 1928 *Friendship* flight, Earhart was engaged to Sam Chapman, a graduate of Tufts University. She broke it off after her return. Though Earhart never gave a reason, her desire to continue working and flying likely influenced her decision. During the 1920s, only 10 percent of married women worked outside the home.[†]

Earhart found a female role model in British feminist Dora Russell. Her 1927 book *The Right to Be Happy* advocated sexual

---

[*] Morrissey, 68.
[†] Dumenil, 113.

equality between men and women, free love, and birth control.*
Earhart agreed with Russell that women were "bred to timidity" and should stand up and take responsibility for themselves.†

During the 1930s, Earhart's promoter, George Palmer Putnam, pursued her and may have proposed as many as six times. (He admitted to being refused "twice at least.")‡ When Earhart finally consented, it was with the understanding that she expected independence. In an unconventional prenuptial letter (see p. 116), she insisted that they each maintain their personal, professional, and sexual independence. Putnam agreed. They were married on February 7, 1931.

Gore Vidal, the son of Earhart's friend Eugene Vidal, believed that his father and Earhart had an affair. While it is possible, he based the assertion largely on the fact that Earhart flew wearing Vidal's boxer shorts. She wore them because they were more convenient in a cockpit's primitive toilet facilities than traditional women's undergarments.§

Defying prevailing custom, Earhart kept her maiden name after marriage. She identified with feminists from the Lucy Stone League, who declared, "My name is the symbol of my identity and must not be lost."¶ George Putnam supported her decision. His wife had made a name for herself, and as her promoter he knew its promotional value.

Earhart believed the culture of the husband as breadwinner

---

 * See Russell.
 † Ibid., 225.
 ‡ Earhart and Backus, 87; Putnam, *Soaring Wings*, 76.
 § Butler, 292, 338. See also Gore Vidal, "Love of Flying," *New York Review*, January 17, 1985, 19, for his perspective on their relationship.
 ¶ Becker, 263.

needed to change. "Women should earn their own salt and men should do their part of the housework. They should help bring up the children too!"[*] (See chapter 10, "On Gender and Age.") Her opinion was outside the mainstream. Twenty-six states had laws prohibiting the employment of married women.[†]

Though she enjoyed children, Earhart and Putnam never had any together. This was likely because it "took too long to make a baby" and because Putnam already had adult children.[‡] Earhart openly supported Margaret Sanger's birth-control movement.[§] From her years in the field of social work and her relationship with her niece and nephew, she formed definite ideas about parenting.

On Marriage

I think what Pidge has done took more courage than my flying did.[1]

Circa June 1929; reaction to her sister's marriage

I am still unsold on marriage, I don't want *anything* all the time. . . . I think I may not ever be able to see marriage except as a cage until I am unfit to work or fly or be active—and of course I wouldn't be desirable then.[2]

Circa 1930

---

[*] "Amelia Earhart, Visitor Here, Discusses Work and Clothes," *Richmond (VA) Times Dispatch*, February 2, 1934.
[†] Koziara, 377.
[‡] Ware, 54.
[§] Letter to Margaret Sanger from Helen Weber, April 4, 1933, Margaret Sanger Papers, Library of Congress, Washington, DC, LCM 50:739A; February 11, 1935, telegram from Earhart to Margaret Sanger, LCM 44:25.

As a sex, women seem to regard matrimony as a highly honorable retreat from business failure.... They think they are after freedom, but what I'm afraid they want is lack of responsibility.[3]

Circa 1931

How does "being in business" (for flying is a business) affect marriage? Obviously I can offer only my own answers—from a woman's viewpoint. It seems to me that the effect of having other interests beyond those exclusively domestic works well. The more one does and sees and feels, the more one is able to do, and the more genuine may be one's appreciation of fundamental things like home, and love, and understanding companionship.[4]

September 1932, *Redbook*

It's about 50–50—marriage and aviation—and I guess one job is about as big as the other.[5]

December 15, 1932, *McKeesport (PA) Daily News*

No human being should "manage" any other human being of normal intelligence. Marriage is a case of mutual responsibility.[6]

January 12, 1934, *Columbus (OH) Citizen*

A woman can make a husband happy and still live her own independent life. And she should.[7]

February 19, 1935, Omaha newspaper

If we begin to think and respond as capable human beings able to deal with and even enjoy the challenges of life, then we surely will have something more to contribute to marriage than our bodies. We must earn true respect and equal rights from men by accepting responsibility.[8]

Date unknown

Why should marriage be a cyclone cellar into which a woman retreats from failure in other spheres?[9]

Date unknown; angry response to a reporter who said, "I still think the smart woman is the one who can get some man able and willing to provide for her."

On Her Engagement to Samuel Chapman

I know what I want to do and I expect to do it married or single.[10]

Circa spring 1928; reaction to those who assumed she would stop flying after marriage

I am no longer engaged to marry. But, you can never tell. If I was sure of the man I might get married tomorrow.[11]

November 23, 1928, *Richmond (VA) Times Dispatch*

On Her Marriage to George Putnam

If I were to become engaged or married to anyone I should certainly make no mystery of it. There would be no percentage for me in trying to hide it.[12]

June 6, 1930, *Los Angeles Times*; on rumors that she was to marry Putnam

> There is not a thing to it at all. . . . Some time in the next 50 years I may be married.[13]

November 10, 1930, *Greensboro (NC) Daily News*; response to reports that she and George Putnam had been issued a marriage license

Dear GPP

There are some things which should be writ before we are married—things we have talked over before—most of them.

You must know again my reluctance to marry, my feelings that I shatter thereby chances in work which means most to me. I feel the move just now as foolish as anything I could do. I know there may be compensations, but have no heart to look ahead.

On our life together I want you to understand I shall not hold you to any midaeval [sic] code of faithfulness to me nor shall I consider myself bound to you similarly. If we can be honest I think the difficulties which arise may best be avoided should you or I become interested deeply (or in passing) in anyone else.

Please let us not interfere with the others' work or play, nor let the world see our private joys or disagreements. In this connection I may have to keep some place where I can go to be myself, now and then, for I cannot guarantee to endure at all times the confinement of even an attractive cage.

I must exact a cruel promise and that is that you will let me go in a year if we find no happiness together.

I will try to do my best in every way and give you that part of me you know and seem to want.[14]

February 7, 1931; Earhart's prenuptial letter. George Putnam agreed to her conditions.

On Marriage, Parenting, and Birth Control 117

Over the broomstick with GP today—stop—Break News Gently to Mother.[15]

February 7, 1931; telegram to her sister, informing the family that she was married

I am much happier than I expected I could ever be in that state. I believe the whole thing was for the best. Of course I go on in the same way as before as far as business is concerned. I haven't changed at all and will only be busier I suppose.[16]

February 22, 1931; letter to her mother

It's not vital, but for flying I'd rather be Miss Earhart. Why drag Mr. Putnam into aviation?[17]

June 21, 1932, *Seattle Daily Times*; on keeping her maiden name

Not that I'm rabid about it, at all, nor a Lucy Stoner, but I think women in aviation should have the same privileges as women who write, and my husband doesn't mind. For social purposes, I think Putnam's a grand name though.[18]

June 25, 1932, *New York Times*; on keeping her maiden name

Ours is a reasonable and contented partnership; my husband with his solo jobs, and I with mine, but the system of dual control works satisfactorily and our work and our play is a great deal together.[19]

Circa 1932–1933

George and I often laughed afterwards when I'd suggest a solo airplane flight would be a good way for women to forget in case they had a misunderstanding with their husbands.[20]

March 17, 1936, *Riverside (CA) Daily Press*; on the rumor that she undertook long fights to solve marital disputes

Perhaps someday we can fly together to some of the remote places of the world—just for fun.[21]

Circa June 1937

On Divorce

I think divorce is a shame.... A marriage that's lasted eighteen years with two children shouldn't be that easy to break up.[22]

Circa 1929; Earhart to George Putnam on his impending divorce from his first wife. He would later marry Earhart.

Many divorces are caused by the complete dependence of the female. At first there is the strong sexual attraction that sometimes masquerades as love. Everything goes well until the first financial crisis jars the man's confidence and threatens the woman's security. The woman can't help. All she can be is dependent, because that's what she has been trained to be. Instead of contributing her own efforts, she becomes accusatory and sullen and the sex drive that passed for love is not longer enough to satisfy either of them.[23]

Circa 1935–1937; from a talk with women at Purdue University

On Parenting

It has been taken for granted that this is a task exclusively for women. But modern sociologists stress the point that the influence of fathers is (or should be) just as important as maternal direction. This doctrine might mean more nursery work for fathers and more going-to-the-office for mothers.[24]

September 1932, *Redbook*

I know from my experience in social service that there is such a thing as too much mother. Let a father take more interest in the child.[25]

Circa 1930s

Anyhow, the theory that it's the man's sole duty to supply the money and the woman's to bring up the children is a survival of the ancient Greek civilization, in which fathers had no parental responsibilities whatever. As a social worker I've seen the disastrous results in families where the children literally don't know their fathers.[26]

February 4, 1933, *Seattle Post-Intelligencer*

Just being a parent doesn't make a person a good parent. Nor do I think we can lay down any black-and-white definition of what makes a good parent. Parenthood exacts different talents in relation to different conditions.[27]

Date unknown

On Birth Control

[I hope] that she has learned enough about anatomy to prevent further trials for a while.[28]

July 1931; letter to her mother, remarking on her sister, who was soon to deliver a second child

Anyway I think he should share the mechanics of being a husband as one [spouse] should not bear the whole responsibility.[29]

February 1932, letter to her mother, remarking on her brother-in-law's responsibility regarding birth control

Amelia Earhart, circa 1928.
Courtesy Library of Congress Prints and Photographs Division.

12.
On Human Qualities and Emotions

Though Amelia Earhart was charismatic and friendly, she wasn't emotionally effusive. She seldom showed irritation or lost her temper. She relied on tremendous self-control to remain calm in the presence of the press, which was such an intrusive presence in her life (see chapter 14, "On Fame and the Press"). The one love poem below illustrates that though she did not often express them, Earhart felt emotions deeply.

On Human Nature

Human nature normally condemns anything new.[1]

Circa 1928

Human intelligence seems to grasp ideas in steps and must work through complicated details to efficient simplicity.[2]

Circa 1928

On Ambition

To want in one's head to do a thing, for its own sake;
to enjoy doing it; to concentrate all of one's energies upon it—
that is not only the surest guarantee of its success. It is also
being true to oneself.[3]

August 1932, *American Magazine*

If there is anything I have learned in life it is this: *If you follow
the inner desire of your heart, the incidentals will take care of
themselves.* If you want badly enough to do a thing, you usually
do it very well; and a thing well done, as society is organized,
usually works out to the benefit of others as well as yourself.[4]

August 1932, *American Magazine*

On Confidence

Confidence is an energizing thing.[5]

July 1929, *Hearst's International-Cosmopolitan*

I do not think one is ever confident. One makes preparations
and takes every precaution possible, but one is never sure. You
can at least hope, and that is about all you can do. There is
always the hope.[6]

May 23, 1932, *West Lancashire Evening Gazette* (Blackpool, England)

On Courage

Courage is the price that Life exacts for granting peace
The soul knows it not, knows no release
From little things:

Knows not the livid loneliness of fear,
Nor mountain heights where bitter joy can hear
The sound of wings.

How can Life grant us boon of living compensate
For gray dull ugliness and pregnant hate
Unless we dare

The soul's dominion? Each time we make a choice, we pay,
With courage to behold restless day,
And count it fair.[7]

> July 1928, *Survey Graphic*; poem submitted to the magazine
> by Marion Perkins without Earhart's approval

The sudden breath of imminent disaster galvanizes; you are coward or hero, you do your best. And I doubt whether, under the tension of crisis, you think much about it. . . . You feel your spiritual pulse in order to ascertain whether it beats to the tune of courage or cowardice.[8]

> September 1932, *Hearst's International-Cosmopolitan*

The actual doing of a dangerous thing, it seems to me, may require little courage. The preparation for it—the acceptance of the inevitable risks involved—may be a far greater test of morale.[9]

September 1932, *Hearst's International-Cosmopolitan*

Women, I think, evince courage quite as much as men, though the manifestations are often different. Special types of courage in women the world has come to take for granted. For instance that connected with childbirth and mother's courage in undertaking a child's upbringing pass unnoticed. Another kind is the self-effacement of modern women who sacrifice "careers" in order to carry on simply as mothers, wives and housekeepers.[10]

September 1932, *Hearst's International-Cosmopolitan*

But I like to fly. So what do I know of courage, anyway?[11]

September 1932, *Hearst's International-Cosmopolitan*

If it took courage I wouldn't have done it.[12]

June 4, 1932; on her solo transatlantic flight

On Desires

Most of the things we want are illogical.[13]

August 1932, *American Magazine*

On Dreams

There must be dreams and the realization of work to do before energy can be effective.[14]

Circa 1932

On Fear

Afraid? No, I wish I had been. I didn't think of it.[15]

July 7, 1928, *New York Times*; on her 1928 transatlantic flight

Obviously I faced the possibility of not returning when I first considered going. Once faced and settled there really wasn't any good reason to refer to it again. After all, even when driving one admits tacitly there is danger, but one doesn't dwell on the result of losing the front wheels or having the rear end fall out on a mountain.[16]

Circa 1928, on fears faced during her first Atlantic crossing

Fear is more or less an emotional attitude.[17]

October 1929, *Hearst's International-Cosmopolitan*

Fear is usually lack of understanding.[18]

November 1929, *Hearst's International-Cosmopolitan*

> Weariness is a great friend of fear.[19]

September 1932, *Hearst's International-Cosmopolitan*

> Fear is a very illogical sort of emotion. All you know is that a horse and buggy is safer than an automobile and probably an ox cart is safer than a horse and buggy, but I didn't see any ox carts drawn up outside this building as I came in. You all drove up in much more dangerous automobiles.[20]

April 21, 1933; address to the Daughters of the American Revolution

On Love

To touch your hand or see your face, today,
Is joy. Your casual presence in a room
Recalls the stars that watched us as we lay

I mark you in the moving crowd
And see again those starts
A warm night lent us long ago.
We loved so then—we love so now.[21]

Unknown date. The poem was one of the few not destroyed in Earhart's Rye, New York, home fire.

On Luck

> The luckiest piece is a good pilot.[22]

February 1, 1933, *News Telegram* (Portland, OR)

Do you think my luck might run out? Do you think luck only lasts so long and then lets a person down?[23]

February 19, 1935

No, I [do] not carry any good luck charms or tokens. I prefer good mechanical work to rabbits' feet.[24]

May 9, 1935, *New York Times*

On Optimism

I should rather be on the side of those who believe anything possible, and who have faith in man's skill in the wings he has found.[25]

October 1929, *Hearst's International-Cosmopolitan*

On Power

Given a little power over another, little natures swell to hideous proportions.[26]

January 31, 1937, letter from Earhart to her sister

On Success

Success in any undertaking, whether it be aeronautical engineering, law, medicine or any other profession, is predicated upon initiative, and the determination to succeed.[27]

October 25, 1932, *Graveraet Weekly* (Marquette, MI)

On Worry

Anxiety is a weight around the neck of any aviator, for it detracts from the concentration and clear thinking necessary for successful flying.[28]

January 23, 1933, *The Campus* (Sarah Lawrence College, Bronxville, NY)

Don't worry until there is something to worry about—then it's usually too late.[29]

February 17, 1935, *Boston Daily Globe*

Worry prevents quick, clear-cut decisions.[30]

March 31, 1935, *Los Angeles Times*

Worry and fatigue are relentless enemies to good judgment.[31]

May 1935, *National Geographic*

Worry retards action, and makes clean-cut decisions impossible. Only by recognizing the hazards can they be overcome.[32]

August 10, 1935, *Chautauqua (NY) Daily*

Hamlet would have been a bad aviator. He worried too much.[33]

Circa 1937

Earhart at a picnic, 1924 or 1925.
Courtesy Purdue University Libraries, Archives and Special Collections.

13.
On Health and Exercise

Amelia Earhart didn't drink or smoke and refused to endorse Lucky Strikes cigarettes after her 1928 Atlantic flight. She changed her mind because she wanted to donate her profits to explorer Admiral Richard Byrd.[*] Her generosity backfired. The ad made it appear that she advocated smoking for women, which at the time was associated with rebelliousness and prostitution.[†]

Earhart's taste in food was simple, both at home and in the air. On long flights, what little she ate included tomato juice, hard-boiled eggs, malted milk tablets, and hot chocolate.[‡]

Raised in an age when girls were discouraged from exerting themselves, Earhart was fortunate that her family was unconventional. They approved of vigorous exercise for girls. She and her sister wore "gymnasium suits," or bloomers, so they could run, jump, and ride horses.

---

[*] Winters, 78–79.
[†] Alexander, 266.
[‡] Earhart, *Last Flight*, 12; Earhart, *20 Hrs., 40 Min.*, 51.

On Alcohol and Prohibition

I was one of the few people who wouldn't drink the medical supply of whiskey.[1]

Circa 1928; on why she was selected to work in a hospital dispensary

It happens that I don't [drink]—it just never seemed worthwhile.[2]

Circa 1928

I feel that alcohol is definitely injurious to the human system.[3]

Date unknown

Everyone knows that alcohol is habit-forming (in the medical sense) and as such cannot be classed with a fondness for pie or baked beans.[4]

Date unknown

People must be shown the evils of the liquor traffic again. . . . I believe better effort can be made in working on constructive programs by which to present reasons for abstinence, such as athletics, etc. for youngsters—for they are the ones who count.[5]

Date unknown

On Smoking

Why shouldn't I smoke if I want to? Whose business is it but mine? . . . There! I smoked! If you really want to know, I probably never will again![6]

Circa 1928. After being criticized for endorsing Lucky Strikes cigarettes, Earhart, in a reactionary mood, tried smoking for the first and last time.

On Food and Cooking

I think I myself can eat anything but oatmeal.[7]

Circa 1933

I don't drink coffee unless I have to.[8]

Circa 1933

I don't like sandwiches. They taste like—mattresses.[9]

Circa 1934–1935

I like and eat simple, plain foods with a widely varied menu. Meat, lots of fruit and vegetables.[10]

February 17, 1935, *Boston Daily Globe*

On Sleep

Oh, I can sleep any time and any where. All people in aviation can. I'd have been dead long ago if I hadn't trained myself to sleep at any time.[11]

October 25, 1932, *Daily Mining Journal* (Marquette, MI)

On Exercise

I am not suggesting that girls jump out of their cribs and begin training, but only that the pleasure from exercise might be enhanced if they knew how to do correctly all the things they can do now without injuring themselves or giving a shock to their elders.[12]

Circa 1933

This is an era of feminine activity. The stay-at-home and the hammock girl are gone. Modern women are strenuously active.[13]

Circa 1934

On Sports

I should like to see professional athletes and professional players in every sport admitted to some contests now open only to those of amateur standing.[14]

December 1932, *Liberty Magazine*. Earhart thought it unfair that professional athletes were barred from the Olympics.

I like to see women enter all sports or activities fearlessly and quietly and do the best they can.[15]

June 30, 1933, *New York Telegram*

On Illness

I am sorry you have had a cold. There is no excuse for it if you will have decent food and rest and some woolen undies in the cold house.[16]

December 8, 1933; letter to her mother

Earhart posing next to a sculpted clay bust, circa 1930s.
Courtesy Purdue University Libraries, Archives and Special Collections.

On Fame and the Press

Amelia Earhart's first experience with the press was an interview about female pilots with the *Boston Daily Globe*, a full year before her first transatlantic crossing.[*] In the years that followed, Earhart developed an open, easygoing style with the press. Reporters found her engaging and surprisingly feminine.[†]

Interviews in newspapers and magazines increased Earhart's fame. They also resulted in paid speaking engagements and commercial endorsements, which in turn financed more flights. So after a long day of travel, speaking to the public at multiple venues, or flying, she made time for the press.

Though she was well liked by the media, Earhart was still the victim of misinformation and downright fabrication. In 1928 reporters claimed that she undertook her first transatlantic flight to save the

---

[*] "Urges Women Take Up Flying," *Boston Daily Globe*, June 26, 1927.
[†] R. Gibson Hubbard, "Scribe Learns Miss Earhart Is Very Feminine," *Oregon Journal* (Portland), February 1, 1933.

family home from foreclosure.[*] The family did not own a home. Later, after she made her solo transatlantic flight, a British newspaper, perhaps seeking to portray her as unsophisticated, quoted her as saying, "Wal, I sure am glad to be here, and gosh, I sure do hope I'll meet the Prince."[†] She denied making the statement.

Earhart had a sense of humor about her celebrity. She called her personal papers "peppers" and marked "bunk" on a file of tributes written to her.[‡] (See chapter 16, "Amelia Earhart on Herself.") She also joked about being mistaken for others.

Sometimes her fame wasn't a joking matter. Spectators rushed the landing strip when she was trying to land. Souvenir hunters stole scarves and tore at her clothing, prompting one reporter to question if "she would not outlive her triumph."[§] Sometimes her protectors were part of the problem. Following her flight from Mexico to Newark, well-meaning police officers attempted to rescue her from an admiring crowd by each grabbing a limb. She was nearly torn in two when they went in different directions.[¶]

On Fame

> I am sure I do not want to be known always merely as the first woman to fly the Atlantic.[1]
>
> June 20, 1928, *New York Times*

---

[*] Earhart, *20 Hrs., 40 Min.*, 39.
[†] Earhart, *The Fun of It*, 86.
[‡] Putnam, *Soaring Wings*, 85, 210.
[§] Winters, 74.
[¶] Butler, 334.

Today I have been receiving offers to go on stage, appear in the movies and to accept numerous gifts ranging from an automobile to a husband. The usual letters of criticism and threats which I have always read celebrities receive have also arrived. And I am caught in a situation where very little of me is free. I am being moved instead of moving.[2]

June 21, 1928, *Boston Herald*

That is the drawback of being a public person—you cannot fall down. People's eyes are on you. Criticism hurts you and sometimes, even if it is unjustifiable, you cannot reply. The pressure of even the warmest praise from persons whose opinions you value loses something by the very excess of it.[3]

June 21, 1928, *New York Times*

I want to become a plain, private person just as quickly as possible.[4]

June 21, 1928, *New York Times*

Because I happen to be the first woman to cross the ocean by air, I am turned into a side show curiosity by many people.[5]

July 12, 1928, *New York Times*

Someone has taken a part of the hood that covers the engine of the machine. I suppose it's hanging in someone's front parlor now. Why they even cut pieces of fabric from the wings of your machine and then ask you to autograph them. Some day a souvenir hound will carry off a vital part of the machine and there will be a crash.[6]

October 12, 1928, *Omaha World Herald*

Personal seclusion all but vanishes. I feel that now, I'm in a position to really appreciate the privacy of the proverbial goldfish.[7]

October 1928, *McCall's*

I was glad to find someone who regarded me as a human being.[8]

Circa 1928; on her meeting with Lady Nancy Astor, who was more interested in Earhart's social work than her flight

I never knew that a "public character" (that, Heaven help me, apparently is my fate since the flight) could be the target of so much mail.[9]

Circa 1928

Autographing, I discover, is a national mania. Requests for photographs, freak suggestions, involved communications from inventors, pathetic appeals, have been numerous.[10]

Circa 1928

Yes, the mail has brought diverse proposals of marriage, and approximations thereof. Perhaps the widespread publication of my photograph has kept the quantity down![11]

Circa 1928

I'm not an actress; I'm a pilot.[12]

Circa 1928; reaction to offers to appear in movies

I believe I never apologized so widely and so consistently for anything in my life, excepting possibly having been born. The title was given, I believe, probably because one or the other of us wasn't a swarthy runt. You understand my dislike of the title isn't because I don't appreciate being compared to one who has abilities such as Colonel Lindbergh has, but because that comparison is quite unjustified.[13]

May 8, 1929; letter to Anne Morrow Lindbergh, explaining her feelings about being called Lady Lindy

So I accept these awards on behalf of the cake baker, and all of those other women who can do some things quite as important, if not more important than flying, as well as in the name of women flying today.[14]

October 6, 1932, *Philadelphia Inquirer*; jibe at an article praising her but asking, "But can she bake cakes?"

I won't have time to sign this letter, so I am asking Mrs. Weber to sign it and send it on.[15]

January 27, 1933; letter to her mother, signed by her secretary

Please don't think me ungracious, but being recognized everywhere and always is sometimes a little tiring. Don't think me a misanthrope, because I'm not. Fundamentally, I like people.[16]

February 3, 1933, *Seattle Daily Times*

And I'm an old story now.[17]

February 3, 1933, *Seattle Daily Times*

To take a year in answering a letter is about my average rate just now. My friends suffer most, because I am continually shoving their letters aside telling myself they will understand the delay while a business correspondent will not. I know my theory is unjust, for I value friends more than I do the butcher, baker, or candlestick maker, worthy souls though they may be. What to do about regulating my life and letters, I know not.[18]

Circa 1934

Mrs. Roosevelt asked me to stay at the White House overnight, then to make it headquarters until Tuesday when I leave for New England.[19]

March 4, 1935; letter to her mother

Strangely, they knew who I was.[20]

April 21, 1935, *New York Times*; on landing in rural Mexico

Please tell Pidge when I wrote her about cancelling a dinner she was planning in Cambridge, I did not mean that GP and I would not be glad to eat at home with *just the family* if she wishes.[21]

November 23, 1935; letter to her mother. She and her husband wanted to dine with her sister and her family, not guests.

You simply can't do anything about such things. People say them and if you deny them, then they assume you're just being coy. So you skip it.[22]

April 29, 1936, *Christian Science Monitor*; on dealing with misleading stories

To injure another's reputation is to stoop very low indeed.[23]

May 2, 1936, *Advocate* (Baton Rouge, LA); reaction to the Senate Air Safety Committee's criticism of pilots

I really have been fortunate, for anyone who has a name in the paper is a target for all sorts of things.[24]

March 20 or 23, 1936; letter to her mother, responding to an accusation by Myrtle Mantz that Earhart was the cause of her marital problems

The fact is that the career of one who indulges in any kind of flying off the beaten path is often complicated. For instance, if one gives out plans beforehand, one is likely to be charged with publicity seeking by those who do not know how difficult it is to escape the competent gentlemen of the press. On the other hand, if one slips away, as I have generally tried to do, the slipper-away invites catcalls from those who earn their living taking photographs.[25]

Circa 1937

Applesauce. We're all puppets. Much as I'd like the check, wash this out. Such drivel.[26]

Date unknown; reaction to a magazine piece that her editor had entirely rewritten to make her look like a hero

I have had things literally stolen off my back.[27]

Unknown date; on being assaulted by fans

On the Press

We have to look nice when reporters come.[28]

Circa 1921; remark made while powdering her nose after a crash

If the Hearst reporter annoys you, wire me and I can have it stopped. Don't worry, but be careful about telling people without Sam.[29]

August 12, 1928; letter to her mother, with advice about dealing with the press. Sam Chapman was her fiancé.

When and if reporters come to you please refer them to Mr. Putnam. Don't even say yes and no if you don't want to. Just say you can add nothing to their tales and to ask me or G. P. P. Tell 'em you know many of my plans but are not divulging.[30]

August 26, 1928; letter to her mother. G.P.P was George Palmer Putnam, her manager and later her husband.

The press introduced me to an entirely new person. It appeared that I was a demi-orphan; my father, I learned, had been dead four years—I saved that clipping for him. One day I read that I was wealthy, the next the sole purpose of my flight was to lift the mortgage from the old homestead—which there isn't any—I mean homestead.[31]

Circa 1928

All right. If they'll be absolutely sure to say the cigarettes were used by the crew. I don't really want to do it, but I want the fifteen hundred bucks to give to Dick.[32]

Circa 1928. As a result of Earhart's reluctant agreement to take part in a Lucy Strikes advertisement, she lost an opportunity to write for *McCall's* magazine, which worried that her endorsement would alienate readers.

Oh no, the photographers are all right. . . . The pictures on the "Friendship" were particularly bad. You see we didn't know anybody would be interested and when people just came in swarms and the photographers started taking pictures, we were excited, and upset and couldn't get our bearings.[33]

October 25, 1932, *Daily Mining Journal* (Marquette, MI)

There were no casualties unless some of them died from fright.[34]

December 14, 1932, *Boston Daily Globe*; on a spurious account that Earhart killed cows when landing in Ireland.

No two had the interview anything alike; in fact, I think they wrote just what they thought I should say.[35]

February 2, 1933, *Oregonian* (Portland); on European reporters

I like the American reporters the best. They know what to ask, and they report what you say.[36]

February 2, 1933, *Oregonian* (Portland)

You know, I shouldn't say it, but I was hungry all the time I was at the White House. I couldn't seem to get enough to eat.[37]

March 11, 1935, *Boston Transcript*. Earhart denied making this statement. Since Eleanor Roosevelt's White House had the reputation for poor food, the press assumed she had been starved.

I assure you there never has been any necessity to raid the icebox.[38]

March 14, 1935; telegram to Eleanor Roosevelt. Earhart sought to assure the First Lady that she hadn't been starved.

It happened I said not *one single word* on the subject. The whole was fabricated out of one reporter's imagination. I can laugh at it now. I only hope some day I can laugh also at the preposterous 'starvation interview' the press has had me give concerning my stay at The White House.[39]

March 14, 1935; draft letter to Eleanor Roosevelt

On my recent flight from Honolulu to Oakland one writer decided that I was bored with my husband. Just how sitting over the Pacific Ocean for 18 hours could alter the situation I do not know, but it is a unique remedy.[40]

Circa June 1935

In all cases, be careful of reporters. They may find you out. Be *cheerful* with them and smile for photographs. The serious face in real life looks sour in print. The grinning face moderately pleasant.

Don't express international opinions. . . . You approve of my flying; you don't know my plans for future; mention any special things that impressed you. (In England talk of English things, France French, etc. Don't praise Westminster in Paris.) *Look on cheerful side* never tell of mishaps, lost baggage, cold mutton chops, runs in your hose, etc.[41]

Circa May 1936; letter to her mother, advising her on dealing with the press while visiting Europe

You know, I feel you newspaper men have pushed me into this. You're the ones who have kept saying and saying that I was going to fly around the world, until finally you've compelled me to think seriously about doing it.[42]

Feb 12, 1937, *Christian Science Monitor*. A reporter countered, "You didn't have to be pushed!" Earhart laughed and admitted that the reporters were right.

Earhart at Purdue University, spring 1937.
Courtesy Purdue University Libraries, Archives and Special Collections.

15. Miscellaneous

On Adventure

I have flown above and below and through other seas of clouds. And ever I find this new world aloft worth the great price of its conquest.[1]

August 1932, *Hearst's International-Cosmopolitan*

Adventure is worth while in itself.[2]

August 1932, *American Magazine*

Adventure is not for novices. It is not for scatterbrains. It is for people who have wanted to do a certain thing, who have wanted it for years more than anything else, and who finally, concentrating on all that above all other beckoning thoughts, have carried it through.[3]

August 1932, *American Magazine*

Everyone has his own Atlantic to fly. Whatever you want very much to do, against the opposition of tradition, neighborhood opinion, and so-called "common sense"—that is an Atlantic.[4]

August 1932, *American Magazine*

Have you ever longed to go to the North Pole? Or smell overripe apples in the sunshine? Or coast down a steep, snow-covered hill to an unknown valley? Or take a job behind a counter selling ribbons, and show people how to sell ribbons as ribbons have never been sold before? Or take a friend by the arm and say, "Forget it—I'm with you forever"? Or, just before a thunderstorm, to turn ten somersaults on the lawn?

If you have some time had a desire like that, you will understand. *The small things that invite us to hop out of the rut mean just as much as flying the Atlantic.* If these are mere daydreams, pass them by. But if they absorb and encompass you, if they get hold of your heart, if they become what the philosopher calls "that obscure inner necessity"—heed them. They are your self.[5]

August 1932, *American Magazine*

You will find the unexpected everywhere as you go through life. By adventuring about, you become accustomed to the unexpected.[6]

Circa 1932

I want to try lots of things—all kinds of things— try them at least once.[7]

Date unknown

It is true that there are no more geographical frontiers to push back—no new lands flowing with milk and honey this side of the moon to promise surcease from man-made ills. But there are economic, political, scientific and artistic frontiers of the most exciting sort awaiting faith and the spirit of adventure to discover them.[8]

Date unknown

On Beauty

Beauty and adventure have a certain value only in spiritual scales. I have the greatest respect for dollars and cents. They are quite important. They pay the rent and the grocer; they buy clothes and satisfy the tax collector. But they are not the final measure of the human spirit.[9]

August 1932, *American Magazine*

The important and exciting thing is to find beauty in living. Of course flight is spectacularly beautiful. But flight is a moment snatched out of a month. What I want inside me all the time is to know the answer to why I'm alive. That's the beauty in living.[10]

August 25, 1935, *Dayton (OH) Daily News*

On Beauty Shops

[I] think beauty parlors are abominable places.[11]

December 12, 1932, *Toronto Daily Star*. Earhart preferred barbershops.

On Being a Pioneer

And if you should find that you are the first *woman* to feel an urge in that direction, what does it matter? Feel it and act on it just the same. It may turn out to be fun. And to me fun is the indispensable part of work.[12]

Circa 1935

It is the most honest motive for the majority of mankind's achievements. To want in one's own heart to do a thing for its own sake; to enjoy doing it; to concentrate all of one's energies upon it—that is not only the surest guarantee of its success, it is also being truly oneself.[13]

Date unknown

On Camels

Camels should have shock absorbers.[14]

Circa June 1937

On Clothes

Everything I've got to wear at present is borrowed, but then I'm not vain.[15]

June 20, 1928, *Repository* (Canton, OH). Earhart brought no extra clothing on her transatlantic flight.

Aviation costumes, except for special flights like this, are a relic of the time when flying was done in primitive planes which did not shield the aviators at all from the wind.[16]

June 22, 1928, *Boston Herald*

> I write of the possibility of flying in ordinary clothes, saving expense and maintaining some attractiveness of costume, because I am lonesome for the companionship of women in aviation.[17]

June 22, 1928, *Boston Herald*

> Do please have Pidge let the children wear socks so they don't look like bumpkins. And why the silly hair ribbon?[18]

April 20, 1933; letter to her mother regarding her nephew's and niece's attire

> Nature is essentially simple, and clothes to be worn in natural surroundings must be completely harmonious with nature.[19]

November 24, 1933, *Omaha World Herald*

> I've seen eyebrows fly up when I mentioned tails on shirts for ladies. But let me tell you many a woman has put her soul in mortal jeopardy out of sheer fury because makers thought it was too crude or impolite—something like that anyway—to supply ladies with tails. I made up my mind that if the wearers of the shirts I designed took time out for any reason to stand on their heads, there would be enough shirt still to stay tucked in![20]

Circa 1933–1934. During the 1930s, women's shirts were relatively short, making it difficult for active women to keep them tucked in.

> I should like to wear a dress that is five years old and which I love; but always, if you design clothes, people look at you with the lynx's eyes and you must dress and dress.[21]

Circa 1933–1934

> I can assure you, sewing is harder than flying.[22]

January 6, 1934, *Newark (NJ) Ledger*

I tried to put the freedom that is in flying into the clothes. And the efficiency too. Some nuts and bolts and screws that are in my Lockheed—I had those copied for fastenings.[23]

February 7, 1934, *Christian Science Monitor*; on her clothing line

I think clothes are only right in proportion as the person wearing them feels at home in them.[24]

February 7, 1934, *Christian Science Monitor*

I hate ruffles.[25]

May 18, 1934, *Springfield (MA) Republican*

I am not doing any designing now. I came to the place where it was either designing or aviation, and I chose aviation.[26]

February 22, 1935, unknown newspaper. Earhart's decision to abandon her clothing line was also motivated by the fact that women could not afford high-end clothing during the Depression.

On Colors

It's a pet theory of mine that color in a drab world can go a long way in stimulating morale.[27]

Circa 1928

On Dancing

By the way, I think dancing can be one of the loveliest pastimes in the world.[28]

Circa 1933

On Death

I just don't like the idea of drowning.[29]

September 1932, *Hearst's International-Cosmopolitan*

Afraid of death? Heavens, yes, nobody wants to die. But you don't think about it [while flying].[30]

October 29, 1932, *Milwaukee Journal*

A fatal accident to a woman pilot is not a greater disaster than one to a man of equal worth. Feminine flyers have never subscribed to the super-sentimental valuation placed upon their needs.[31]

Circa 1933; reflecting on the death of Marvel Crosson during the 1929 air derby

When I go, I would like best to go in my plane. Quickly.[32]

September 26, 1937, *Boston Daily Globe*

Some day, I'll get bumped off. There's so much to do, so much fun here. I don't want to go.[33]

Circa 1937

If I *should* bop off, it will be doing the thing I've always wanted most to do. Being a fatalist yourself, you know the Man with the little black book has a date marked down for us when our work here is finished.[34]

Circa 1937; to fellow pilot Louise Thaden

On Exploration

Of course it is fun to try something new. I supposed that's the thrill of exploration, the joy of pioneering, of seeing for the first time from the sea or from the air a land that no one else has seen.[35]

January 3, 1936, *Jewish Chronicle* (Newark, NJ)

On Family

The cooperation of one's family and close friends is one of the greatest safety factors a fledgling flyer can have.[36]

Circa 1933

On Her Secret

I'll be back in N.Y. about the 14th and will probably come north to see you and unfold the *great secret*.[37]

May 6, 1936; letter to her mother. Some biographers believe Earhart was pregnant. She was more likely she referring to the surprise European trip she had planned for her mother.

On History and Artifacts

The malady of collecting souvenirs seems to be universal in its scope—but one grandchild's loss is another one's gain.[38]

Circa 1933; reflecting on how the *Friendship* was stripped by souvenir seekers

On Hunting

I held out, as always, against killing for killing sake. To acquire land, to protect property, or livestock, or to provide museums with specimens for scientific purposes, seems to me to be the only possible justification for slaughter. Even those excuses should be controlled, even more, than they are today, lest animals face extinction on one coast or another.[39]

December 1934, *Outdoor Life*

On Life

In my life I had come to realize that when things were going very well indeed it was just the time to anticipate trouble. And, conversely, I learned from pleasant experience that at the most despairing crisis, when all looked sour beyond words, some delightful "break" was apt to lurk just around the corner.[40]

Circa 1937

On Mechanics

The best mascot is a good mechanic.[41]

Date unknown

On Motorcycle Police Officers

They are so good to look at.[42]

Circa 1928

On Movies

I think it's too bad when aviation movies depend for their excitement upon plane wrecks, lost flyers, and all that sort of thing. Perhaps that's good drama, perhaps it isn't; but it certainly isn't modern aviation.[43]

June 1933, *Screenland*

It's true that there haven't been any pictures centering around women's part in aviation, while men's achievements have been glorified over and over. And while I'm not prepared to speak about dramatic values, it seems to me the more progressive thing would be legitimately to feature women if such romance of aviation is to be found—in the tale of its heroic beginnings and its growth and expansion.[44]

June 1933, *Screenland*

On Photography

Having only two hands and two feet, I took no pictures on the Atlantic solo flight.[45]

April 1933, *Vanity Fair*

Having lived a peripatetic life—never longer than four years in one place, with frequent lengthy excursions away from that, I suppose pictures mean more to me than to some people. They are stabilizers on a shifting world and tend to keep records straight and memories fresh.[46]

April 1933, *Vanity Fair*

On Places

On Africa

Africa smells. The same smell pervades Dakar as St. Louis. To me it seemed a sort of strong human tang of people, quite different from the aromas of South American cities which are those of fruit, fish, meat and growing things—sometimes overgrown![47]

Circa 1937

Seeing the majesty of these natives I asked myself what many must have asked before: What have we in the United States done to these proud people, so handsome and intelligent in the setting of their own country?[48]

Circa 1937; on Dakar, Senegal

On Enid, Oklahoma

This part of the state is one of the prettiest I have passed over.... Enid can be seen for a long distance, and the town itself is very beautiful.[49]

Circa 1931, *Enid (OK) Morning Times*

On England

Its countryside is every bit as beautiful as the books always say. I seem to remember a legend about the English people being aloof and perhaps a little cold; but nobody could have surpassed the hospitality and friendliness to me.[50]

June 22, 1928, *New York Times*

On France

Where Frenchmen are, there is also good food.[51]

Circa 1937

On Germany

They are not all changed as yet. I wonder whether they *will* ever change?[52]

Circa 1918–1919; on German militarism

On Mexico

Mexico is four times as civilized as Newark.[53]

May 9, 1935, *Trenton (NJ) Evening Times*; reaction to being mobbed at the Newark airport after her return from Mexico

On Newfoundland

The cruelty of country and climate is surely a contrast to the kind hearts of the people of Newfoundland.[54]

Circa 1928

On Texas

I do love the space of this country.[55]

December 8, 1933; letter to her mother

On Toledo, Ohio

Toledo is beautiful from the air. I don't believe I have ever seen anything more lovely than the view of the river, the bay and Lake Erie.[56]

July 23, 1928, *Toledo (OH) News-Bee*

On Religion

Don't think for an instant I would ever become an atheist or even a doubter nor lose faith in the church's teachings as a whole. That's impossible. But you must admit there is [a] great deal radically wrong with the methods and teaching and results today. Probably no more than yesterday, but the present stands up and waves its paws at me I see—can't help it. It is not the clergy nor the church itself nor the people that are narrow, but the outside pressure that squeezes them into a routine.[57]

Circa September 1919; letter to her mother

I didn't say I believed the Arabic doctrines. I'm just interested in what people in other parts of the world believe.[58]

Circa 1921; responding to questions about her interest in Islam

I think of God as a symbol for good—thinking good, identifying as good in everybody and everything. This God I think of is not an abstraction, but a vitalizing, universal force, eternally present, and at all times available.[59]

Circa 1935

On Urban and Rural Children

The urban child is boldly independent, while the children of remote communities have so little contact with the outer world that they are self-conscious with strangers.[60]

Circa 1928

On Her Will and "Popping Off" Letters

My regret is I leave just now. In a few years, I feel I could have laid by something substantial for so many new things were opening for me.[61]

May 20, 1928; last will and testament, written before her first transatlantic crossing

Even tho I lost the adventure was worthwhile. Our family tends to be too secure. My life has really been very happy and I didn't mind contemplating its end in the midst of that.[62]

May 20, 1928; "popping off" letter to her mother, written in case she died on the 1928 transatlantic crossing

Hooray for the last grand adventure. I wish I had won but it was worthwhile anyway. I have no faith we'll meet anywhere again, but I wish we might.[63]

May 20, 1928; "popping off" letter to her father, written in case she died on the 1928 transatlantic crossing

I have tried to play for a large stake, and if I succeed all will be well. If I don't, I shall be happy to pop off in the midst of such an adventure. My only regret would be leaving you and mother stranded for a while.[64]

June 5, 1928, *New York Times*

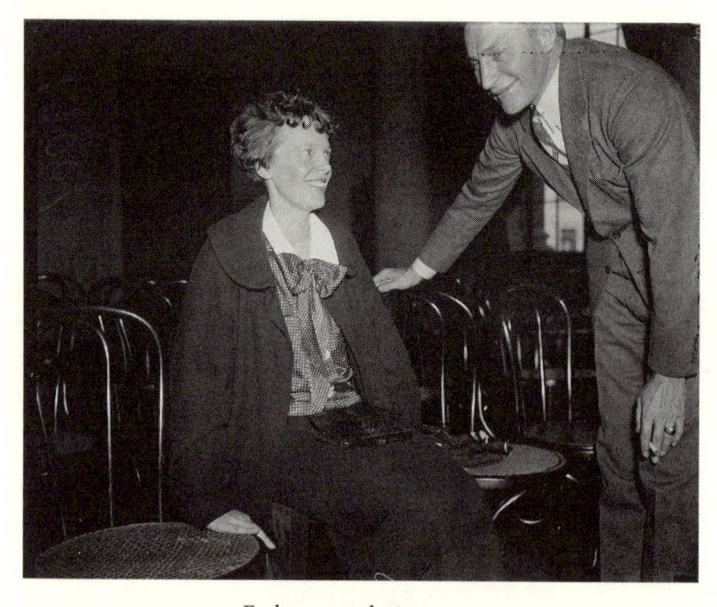

Earhart seated, circa 1936.
Courtesy Library of Congress Prints and Photographs Division.

16.
Amelia Earhart on Herself

Despite her many accomplishments, Amelia Earhart was modest, both about her flying career and her fame. In personal interactions as well as interviews, she frequently made light of her records and accomplishments.

> Did I tell you I have a reputation for brains?[1]

October 25, 1916; letter to her mother, while Earhart was attending the Ogontz School

> My nickname here is either Meelie or Butterball—butter for short.[2]

November 1917; letter to her mother. "Butterball" was an ironic reference to her slight figure.

> Personally, aviation started as a mere sport with me. It has taken more and more of my thoughts until it is a major interest; although not a dominant one.[3]

June 20, 1928, *New York Times*

> I wish I knew radio. I could help a lot.[4]

Circa June 1928. Earhart recognized her lack of skills on the *Friendship* flight. Many experts think this deficiency contributed to her 1937 disappearance.

> I never really thought of it, and I don't know yet that I look at all like Lindbergh.[5]

July 6, 1928, *Christian Science Monitor*; on being called Lady Lindy

> I'm only a social worker on a bat.[6]

July 8, 1928, *Plain Dealer* (Cleveland, OH). "On a bat" is a slang term meaning on a spree or binge.

> I don't profess or pretend to be a flier. I am just an amateur, a dub, flying around the country for personal amusement.[7]

September 15, 1928, *New York Times*

> I was—and am—a social worker, for whom, generally speaking, aviation has been a luring avocation. It just happened that providentially my vacation and the chance to fly the Atlantic came at the same time. I took them both.[8]

October 1928, *McCall's*

> [My] I.Q. is low enough to insure natural cheerfulness.[9]

Circa 1928

> I am by nature a person who experiments.[10]

Circa 1931

I couldn't begin to tell you all the things I tried my hand at.... But looking back, I see so clearly that one thing led to another, and that each thing I did gave me something which is very useful to me today.[11]

Circa 1931

And I am the kind of person that has to do the thing herself in order to be sure in her own mind just what its merits are.[12]

Circa 1931

Why, yes, I think I was interested in mechanical things as a child. But that, to me, isn't nearly so important as the fact that later on I got out and did *something*.[13]

Circa 1931

The moment I saw the planes in flight and heard the rhythmic whirr of their motors, I felt the call of the air.[14]

January 1932, *Illustrated Love Magazine*

I have always enjoyed doing new things, *first-time* things.... Whether it was considered "the thing to do" or not was irrelevant.[15]

August 1932, *American Magazine*

I am not a torchbearer. I fly because I like it.[16]

December 9, 1932, *Springfield (MA) Daily Republican*

But you know, four-fifths of those so-called firsts of mine should be wiped out. They don't mean any more than the parsley on a lamb chop.[17]

December 12, 1932, *Toronto Daily Star*

It's partly a determination to break away from this inbred timidity which has made me do some of the things I have done.[18]

December 12, 1932, *Toronto Daily Star*. Earhart admired British feminist Dora Russell, whose book *The Right to Be Happy* claimed that women were raised with "inbred timidity."

I'm really very fortunate because flying is both my business and my pleasure. I've got a job I love.[19]

Circa 1932

Probably, as you say, I'll be forgotten; but I'll be happier tomorrow if I don't rush today into something I don't want to do.[20]

Circa 1932–1935; response to Universal Studios director Carl Laemmle's assertion that if she didn't star in his film, "In a year—perhaps a few months—you'll be forgotten."

Some day—if they'll let me play my unromantic self, slacks, engine grease and all.[21]

Circa 1932–1935; on appearing in a movie as herself

I studied to be a doctor. I never graduated from any school and I hold no degrees except an honorary one. It's because I thought I could better educate myself by choosing my own subjects rather than by concentrating on any special field.[22]

February 3, 1933, *Seattle Daily Times*

Whether I'm a good flyer is debatable. Whether or not I'm a finished fisherman isn't. I'm not.[23]

December 1934, *Outdoor Life*

You see, my interest in aviation goes into every part of the industry. It is not flying alone. To be interested in pilots alone would be like being interested alone in the engineer in the railroad industry.[24]

Circa 1934–1935

I realize that I have made a serious mistake, a great error. I was born a mere *woman* instead of being a man![25]

January 2, 1935; response to criticism that her Hawaii-to-California flight was ill conceived and dangerous

I fly a little and I write a little.[26]

January 14, 1935, *San Diego Union*

My contributions to aviation have proved very little from a scientific standpoint. I have only proved that a woman can accomplish just as much as a man.[27]

February 14, 1935, *Akron (OH) Beacon*

I don't consider myself a hero. I don't think I've done anything out of the ordinary.[28]

February 22, 1935; newspaper interview

I'll keep on flying until I achieve in aviation everything that men have achieved. I'm going to equal their records and then some.[29]

May 24, 1935, *Boston Daily Globe*

My only reason for flying is my own desire to do so and my love of it.[30]

August 10, 1935, *Chautauqua (NY) Daily*

Right now, I've stopped being a personality in order to be a person. I don't want to be anything but myself for the next little while.[31]

August 25, 1935, *Dayton (OH) Daily News*

My tastes? I enjoy the legitimate theater, especially Katherine Cornell. I like every outdoor activity—swimming, motoring, and horse-back riding. . . . I like poetry. . . . I have done some settlement work. But really my whole story is the Story of Aviation.[32]

August 1935, *The Farmer's Wife*

I've been mistaken for many persons, seldom myself. I've been congratulated on swimming the English channel and mistaken for virtually everybody, from Mabel Walker Willebrandt to Col. Lindbergh's grandmother.[33]

March 5, 1936, *Times Advocate* (Baton Rouge, LA). Willebrandt was a famous female lawyer.

Aviation is my vocation and my avocation. I should rather help the industry than progress myself.[34]

September 15, 1936; telegram to Eleanor Roosevelt protesting the firing of Eugene Vidal, director of the Bureau of Air Commerce

I have always done that kind of flying, in which an element of danger is present.[35]

March 26, 1937, *Los Angeles Times*

I've always been the restless type. I've always wanted to be on the go, and when I start I want to get to my destination in a hurry.[36]

July 13, 1937, *Omaha (NE) World Herald*

It is hard to be old—so hard. I'm afraid I'll hate it. Hate to grow old. I think probably, GP, that I'll not live—to be old.[37]

Unknown date

However, flying does not require all of my time. I have a husband, a home, and I like to read and sew.[38]

Unknown date, *Huntington (IN) Herald Press*

On Her Appearance

You know I'm taller than anyone else except Mrs. Roosevelt.[39]

January 25, 1934, *Boston Daily Globe*; on her height of 5'7"

I've never been on a diet. My weight is 122 pounds, which is probably under the weight tables one sees on scales.[40]

February 17, 1935, *Boston Daily Globe*

Well, that's why I took up aviation; I did it simply because I wasn't beautiful and was determined to do something to offset it![41]

July 13, 1937, *Omaha (NE) World Herald*

Criticism, good-natured and otherwise, sometimes becomes a bit personal. I suspect it it's always an open season for aviatrix. My hair, and the state it's in, is apt to be an object of uncomplimentary comment.[42]

Circa 1937

Earhart and Eleanor Roosevelt, 1935.
Courtesy Library of Congress Prints and Photographs Division.

Amelia Earhart on Others

Amelia Earhart was deeply interested in people but was not one to gossip or share her impressions of individuals. When she did, her comments were perceptive and kind. She was extremely supportive of other pilots, male and female, and put in a good word for them whenever possible.

King Albert I of Brussels (1875–1934)

I found our host not at all "kingly" in any conventional sense, but with a spirit that became him better than a crown.[1]

Circa spring 1932

Amy Otis Earhart (1869–1962), her mother

She has remained sold [on my flying], and it was her regret she wasn't with me on the trans-Atlantic flight, if I would go.[2]

Circa 1928

I think the newspaper clipping makes you look as if you were addicted to the bottle.[3]

Unknown date; note teasing her mother

Edward Earhart (1872–1930), her father

He was an aristocrat as he went—all the weakness gone with a little boy's brown puzzled eyes.[4]

October 2, 1930; letter to her mother, about his death

Anne Morrow Lindbergh (1906–2001), writer and pilot

Perhaps no woman flyer is more interesting than Anne Lindbergh.[5]

Circa 1932

She is an extremely feminine, genuine personage, without mannerism, pretenses or superiorities. . . . Hers is a reticence of genuine modesty without aloofness. She likes flying, not as a personage, but as a person.[6]

Unknown date

Charles Lindbergh (1902–1974), pilot

The difference is that he is Swedish, and I just look Swedish.[7]

February 2, 1934, *Richmond (VA) Times Dispatch*

There's a mania to manhandle Lindbergh. No man has ever been treated as he has.[8]

Unknown date

Myrtle Mantz

Poor old Myrtle Mantz had to get nasty in the trial. The only two women she had not driven away from Paul paid for their loyalty by being dragged into a divorce suit. The silly accusations fell of their own weight and I cannot but feel she will eventually do something so disgraceful that the world will know what she is. Because, of course, after her self inflicted publicity she will be watched.[9]

March 1936; letter to her mother. Myrtle Mantz accused Earhart of breaking up her marriage to Paul Mantz. The scandal made newspapers nationwide.

Ruth Nichols (1901–1960), pilot

She is an excellent flier. . . . I think her chances of getting across are excellent. The women have to prove that they can accomplish things.[10]

June 1, 1931, *World-Herald* (Omaha, NE); on her friend's attempt at a transatlantic crossing. Nichols crashed but survived.

Wiley Post (1898–1935), pilot

There should be some sort of fund for men like Wiley. His span of most useful years does not last so long. He should not be required to spend most of his time scraping together the money necessary for his achievements.[11]

February 19, 1935, *Omaha (NE) World Herald*; comment made a few months before Wiley Post and Will Rogers died together in a plane crash. Earhart could relate to Wiley's constant scramble to raise money.

I'd have been willing to fly anywhere with Wiley Post. He was one of the best. Remember, he was what you might call pioneering.[12]

August 19, 1935, *Boston Daily Globe*; on the death of Post and Will Rogers in a plane crash

Of course, I shall always think of Wiley as being the bravest of the brave.[13]

October 1935, *Forum*

Dorothy Binney Putnam Upton Blanding Palmer (1888–1982), George Putnam's first wife

I'd like to dedicate my book to you, Dottie, if you think it's good enough, and if you don't, I won't. But I'd like to.[14]

August 17, 1928. Earhart stayed with the Putnams while she wrote *20 Hrs., 40 Min.* Dorothy and George would later divorce and Earhart would marry George.

George Palmer Putnam (1887–1950), Earhart's husband

I just didn't like him.[15]

Circa 1928; on her first impression of him

We came to depend on each other, yet it was only friendship between us, or so—at least—I thought at first. At least I didn't admit even to myself that I was in love. . . . but at last that time came, I don't know when it happened, when I could deceive myself no longer. I couldn't continue telling myself that what I felt for G. P. was only friendship. I knew I had found the one person who could put up with me.[16]

January 1932, *Illustrated Love Magazine*

While Mr. Putnam could not have said "Thou shalt not," any more than I could say it to him, he could have been so disagreeable that I would not have taken off on that flight, but he had confidence in my confidence.[17]

June 28, 1932, *Daily Item* (Chester, NY)

He is such a good sport about my flying. If he hadn't been I never could have made that ocean flight.[18]

October 25, 1932, *Morning Journal* (Marquette, MI)

I think my husband has always found a sort of grim satisfaction—a species of modern martyrdom—in being, for once, the male left behind while the female fares forth adventure-bound, thus turning topsy-turvy the accepted way of the world in such matters.[19]

Circa 1937

My husband is a practicing believer in wives doing what they do best, and an approving and helpful partner in all my projects.[20]

Unknown date

Eleanor Roosevelt (1884–1962), First Lady

I think the example which is set by the first lady of the land has done more to help air transportation than any single factor, the fact that Mrs. Roosevelt flies and enjoys it.[21]

April 21, 1933; speech to the Daughters of the American Revolution.
The evening before the speech, Earhart took the First Lady on a night flight over the nation's capital.

Franklin Delano Roosevelt (1862–1945), president

He has fought against odds to reduce human misery. He has realized that obsolescence can affect parts of the machinery of government just as it does the machinery of industry.[22]

Circa 1936

Earhart and President Calvin Coolidge, November 2, 1928.
Courtesy Library of Congress Prints and Photographs Division.

18.

Others on Amelia Earhart

After her first transatlantic crossing in 1928, Earhart's public exploits, fame, and success in a male-dominated field caused people to make assumptions about her. Reporters steeled themselves, preparing to greet an aggressive, domineering egomaniac. Instead she was relatively meek, but she was also a vibrant and engaging woman.

An Omaha newspaper reporter mused, "Perhaps it is her attractive person, perhaps her soft modulated voice, or again her delightful sense of humor—simple humor and largely at her own expense—that enthralls all who hear her."[*]

It wasn't Earhart's untimely death that consigned her to hagiography. Most of the comments below were made before her plane was lost in 1937. Despite intense media scrutiny, she was genuinely well liked. Those who criticized her did so, more often than not, because they detested her pushy husband, George Putnam. Others thought that other pilots deserved fame more than she, or felt that she was overly ambitious for a woman.

---

[*] "Omaha Likes Little Amelia," *Omaha World Herald*, February 21, 1935

The Aeroplane, British magazine

She is thirty-six years old and ought to know better.[1]

January 16, 1935; regarding her flight from Hawaii to California

C. B. Allen (1896–1971), *New York Herald Tribune* correspondent

It was, undoubtedly, something of a shock to discover that the "gal" with whom [the mechanics] had to deal not only was an exceptionally pleasant and reasonable human being who "knew her stuff," but that she knew exactly what she wanted done, and had sense enough to let them alone while they did it. There was an almost audible clatter of chips falling off skeptical masculine shoulders.[2]

Circa spring 1937; on Earhart's preparations for her round-the-world flight

Lady Nancy Witcher Langhorne Astor (1879–1964), member of Parliament

She has charm, intelligence and, above all, character.[3]

June 28, 1928, *New York Times*

Florence "Pancho" Barnes (1901–1975), pilot

She was a goddamned robot. Putnam would wind her up and she'd go and do what he said.[4]

Unknown date

Boston Globe

Amelia Earhart is giving courage to thousands of girls because she has done what only one other person has accomplished in the most spectacular enterprise in which human creatures engage.... The girl who is being repressed will be able to point to the curly head of the woman who has flown the Atlantic alone. That will be a help toward liberation.[5]

June 30, 1932, on her solo transatlantic crossing

Arthur Brisbane (1864–1936), newspaper editor

This flight by Mrs. Earhart Putnam will let them know something about American girls. Nobody can estimate the terrific energy possessed by American women, or how great a loss it is to the world that so little of that energy is made useful.[6]

May 22, 1932, *San Diego Union*; on Earhart's solo transatlantic crossing

Rear Admiral Richard E. Byrd (1888–1957), explorer

America should be proud of Amelia Earhart. She is a very gallant lady—at home in the universe and unafraid![7]

October 1928, *McCall's*

Amelia Putnam is an extraordinary person. I know of no man who has more courage than she. There is absolutely no excuse for a man to feel proud about his exploits as a male.[8]

May 22, 1932, *Boston Daily Globe*

Hattie W. Caraway (1878–1950), Arkansas senator

She was a woman who symbolized to a remarkable degree the courage, the pioneering spirit and the broad achievements of American womanhood. She had only 39 years of life, but into those years she poured a spirit so untrammeled that the world of men and women has a truer conception of what heights a woman may reach when she girds herself to competition on an equal footing with men.[9]

May 27, 1938; speech to the United States Senate

Carrie Chapman Catt (1859–1947), suffragist

Your splendid achievement reflects glory on American womanhood.[10]

June 19, 1932; telegram to Earhart on solo her transatlantic crossing

Jacqueline Cochran (1906–1980), pilot

To put your wife in the shade.[11]

Circa 1936; response to George Putnam, who questioned Cochran about her ambitions. Despite her comment, Cochran admired Earhart.

Amelia was my inspiration.[12]

Unknown date

Calvin Coolidge (1872–1933), president

To you the first woman to span the North Atlantic by Air[,] the great admiration of myself and the United States for your flight.[13]

June 18, 1932; letter to Earhart

Phil Cooper, Earhart's dry cleaner

I knew you'd do it. I never lost a customer.[14]

December 1932, *Pictorial Review*

Amy Otis Earhart (1869–1972), Earhart's mother

I think she's too smart to try it.[15]

June 21, 1928, *Boston Herald*; on her first transatlantic crossing

Well, now that it's all over, I'll have a chance to catch up on my mending.[16]

July 19, 1928, *New York Times*; on the completion of her first transatlantic crossing

She no sooner finishes one thing than she's mentally miles ahead on another adventure.

September 25, 1932, *Richmond (VA) Times Dispatch*

I felt the only time I had a chance to talk to her was when I was holding on to her coat tails.[17]

Date unknown

Edward S. Earhart (1867–1930), father

Meely [her pet name] has a wonderful brain. She'll go far.[18]

Circa 1921

I am at a loss to explain. I know that she doesn't want the publicity or the glory.[19]

June 18, 1928, *Los Angeles Times*; reaction to her first transatlantic flight

I do not consider her an adventurous person.[20]

June 18, 1928, *Los Angeles Times*

When I first discovered she was flying I told her I was strongly against it.[21]

June 19, 1928, *Tampa (FL) Tribune*

Amelia, I knew you would do your stuff.[22]

June 19, 1928, *Los Angeles Times*; on her first transatlantic crossing

Bess Furman (1894–1969), journalist

Looking as much like Lindbergh as a woman can look like a man, and hating the resemblance, Amelia breezily gathered up good will among news writers as easily as Lindbergh collected antagonism.[23]

Circa 1949

Dr. Lillian Moller Gilbreth (1878–1972), psychologist and industrial engineer

Miss Earhart has shown us that all God's chillun got wings.[24]

Circa 1932

Amy Phipps Guest (1873–1959), pilot and sponsor of the 1928 *Friendship* flight

Miss Earhart is a very high type of girl who made the flight for the progress of aviation and for no egotistical, selfish reasons. She is, as we say in aviation, "a regular fellow."[25]

June 20, 1928, *Christian Science Monitor*

Fanny Hearst (1889–1968), novelist

Her bright transcendent spirit of valor, duty and idealism hovers over and blesses the century that contained her.[26]

November 22, 1937, *New York Times*

Herbert Hoover (1874–1964), president

You have demonstrated not only your own dauntless courage but also the capacity of women to match the skill of men in carrying through the most difficult feats of high adventure.[27]

May 21, 1932; telegram to Earhart

Miss Earhart has been modest and good-humored. Her accomplishments combine to place her in spirit with great pioneering women to whom every generation of Americans has looked up with admiration for their firmness of will, their strength of character, and their cheerful spirit of comradeship in the work of the world.... Her success has not been won by the selfish pursuit of a purely personal ambition, but as part of a career generously animated by a wish to help others to share in the rich opportunities of life, and by a wish also to enlarge those opportunities by expanding the powers of women.[28]

June 21, 1932

Lou Henry Hoover (1874–1944), First Lady

If a girl was to fly across the Atlantic alone and so, in a sense, represent America before the world, how nice it is that it was such a person as Miss Earhart. She is poised, well bred, lovely to look at and so intelligent and sincere.[29]

June 21, 1932

Sir Anthony Jenkinson (1912–1989), British journalist

Clearly hers is a mental rather than a physical courage, giving effect, not to bulging muscles and a philosophy of reckless, senseless daring, but rather to abundant confidence, poise and a firm, purposeful character.[30]

February 5, 1935

Sinclair Lewis (1885–1951), novelist

This January, 1935, Amelia Earhart was flashing from Hawaii to Oakland, and ending forever not only the myth that we are softer than our pioneer forbears, but also the myth that women have less endurance and resoluteness than men.[31]

May 1935, *Good Housekeeping*

Anne Morrow Lindbergh (1906–2001), writer and pilot

She is the most amazing person—just as tremendous as C[harles], I think. It startles me how much alike they are in breadth. C doesn't realize it, but he hasn't talked to her as much. She has the clarity of mind, impersonal eye, coolness of temperament, balance of a scientist. Aside from that, I like her.[32]

January 13–14, 1930; letter from Anne Morrow Lindbergh to her sister

[She is] a shaft of white coming out of a blue room.[33]

Circa 1933–1935

Charles Lindbergh (1902–1974), pilot

I heard Amelia made a very good landing—once.[34]

June 21, 1932

Commodore Harry Manning (1897–1974), navigator

Amelia Earhart was something of a prima donna. She gave the impression of being humble and shy; but she really had ego, and could be as tough as nails when the occasion required it. I got fed up with her bull-headedness several times.[35]

Date unknown

Myrtle Harvey Mantz,
wife of aviation technician Paul Mantz

I know I am insanely jealous and upset, but I believe if Miss Earhart would take her clothes and leave our house we would have a much better chance of getting along.[36]

March 3, 1936, *Trenton (NJ) Evening Times*. Myrtle Mantz, in the middle of a divorce dispute, tried to implicate Earhart. Earhart had stayed at the Mantz home, but not without her husband.

Marie Mattingly Meloney (1878–1943), journalist

No generation which could produce Amelia Earhart can be called a lost generation.[37]

Circa 1934

Grace Muriel Earhart Morrissey (1899–1998), Earhart's sister

She certainly would have been a different person if she had a baby to tie her down.[38]

Unknown date

New York Post

We think it an almost entirely silly and useless performance. About all she has proved is that well-known phenomenon of nature that a girl can't jump quite as far as a boy can.[39]

May 21, 1932; on her solo transatlantic crossing. Earhart landed in Ireland, while Lindbergh made it to Paris.

New York Times

She was in rebellion against a world which had been made for women, too safe, too unexciting. She wanted to dare all that a man would dare.... For hers was a deeply feminine valor that could look life and death in the eye as unflinchingly as any man.[40]

July 20, 1937; editorial

Ruth Nichols (1901–1960), pilot

I am absolutely sincere when I say that I don't know of any woman in the United States who has done more for aviation than Amelia Earhart.... I believe that Miss Earhart has crystallized in the minds of the public a realization that women can fly.[41]

June 28, 1932, *Daily Item* (Chester, NY)

Frederick J. Noonan (1893–1937), navigator

She is the only flier I would care to make such a trip with, because in addition to being a fine companion, she can take hardship as well as a man, and work like one.[42]

June 20, 1937; letter from Noonan to his wife

Blanche Noyes (1900–1981), pilot

She was one of the most humane persons I ever had known. If she liked you, she liked you. If she didn't, she let you alone, because there was nothing catty about her. I don't think there was a jealous bone in Amelia's body.[43]

Unknown date

Phoebe Omlie (1902–1975), pilot

She is all woman and one that the other women of America can proudly put up as an example of their contribution to the progress of this great generation.[44]

Unknown date

Alice Stokes Paul (1885–1977), suffragist

Certainly Miss Earhart herself has demonstrated the fallacy of that old idea of women's physical inferiority which we meet on a thousand fronts every day.[45]

November 8, 1935, *New York Times*

Marion Perkins, Earhart's supervisor at Denison House

She is modest, frank, honest and has a complete lack of any quality that makes for sensationalism; and she has a keen insight into child life.[46]

June 19, 1928, *New York Times*

David Binney Putnam (1913–1992), stepson

She looked like a bag of bones in a bathing suit, she was so thin, but she had beautiful clothes and she knew how to wear them. When she was all dressed up, she didn't look like she had *tried* to be all dressed up.[47]

Unknown date

Dorothy Binney Putnam Upton Blanding Palmer (1888–1982), ex-wife of George Putnam

I have seldom encountered a more thoroughly delightful person. She is most extraordinarily cool and self-possessed. Although I saw her during the trying time when the hop was being delayed from day to day, her poise was remarkable. . . . She is a lady in the very best sense of the word, an educated and cultivated person with a fine, healthy sense of humor. And a girl easy to look at too.[48]

June 18, 1928, *New York Times*

George is absorbed in Amelia and admires and likes her. Maybe he's in love with her.[49]

Circa summer of 1928. Though Dorothy was already having an affair, she was displeased about George's interest in Earhart.

George's obsession for A. E. and his clamor to be with her every minute, all day, every day on one pretext or another will give me the very excuse I need for a separation—if not a divorce.[50]

Fall 1928

I released him just so he could marry her. She's to get my husband, my house, my lovely garden—but not my furniture.[51]

December 20, 1929

Too bad they just don't up and marry and have it over with. They'll fight like cats and dogs in a year. She's stubborn and cold bloodedly cruel and she'll soon tire of his indigestion and rotten, vile temper.[52]

November 14, 1930. George Putnam married Earhart on February 7, 1931.

The most delightful person I ever met.[53]

February 8, 1931, *Omaha World Herald*

She's done it! She flew across to Ireland. Solo. World Attention![54]

May 20, 1932; diary entry

Frances Faulkner Putnam (1857–1936), Earhart's mother-in-law

And the thing I'm most proud of about the trip is that she earned all the money herself to finance it.[55]

September 22, 1932, *Press-Scimitar* (Memphis, TN); on Earhart's 1932 transatlantic crossing

George Palmer Putnam (1887–1950), Earhart's husband

She was as sore as a wet hen! She didn't like me one bit and she didn't take much pains to conceal her dislike.[56]

Circa April 1928. Earhart didn't appreciate being made to wait hours in Putnam's office.

To a favorite aeronaut about to embark on a new adventure.[57]

Circa 1930; Putnam's book dedication to Earhart

To marry Miss Amelia Earhart would be swell.[58]

February 8, 1931, *Boston Daily Globe*

Stop her? Don't be silly! I'll aid and abet her.[59]

February 18, 1931, *Greensboro (NC) Record*. As her promoter, Putnam did not discourage Earhart from flying.

I have licked her at plenty of things. If she were a gloating feminist, always harping on about her career and her success and never letting me get an oar into the conversation, I should probably have to sock her.[60]

February 8, 1932, *New York World Telegram*

This is her stunt. She is doing it under her own name, Amelia Earhart. That's the name she made for herself.[61]

May 21, 1932, *New York World Tribune*

I knew that if any woman could do this great feat she was the one; but I have been in deadly fear of the terrors of the Atlantic all night.[62]

May 22, 1932, *Sunday Mail* (London); Putnam's reaction to her solo transatlantic crossing

As her husband, I guess it would be proper to remark I hope it doesn't become a habit.[63]

May 22, 1932, *Tampa (FL) Sunday Tribune*; reflecting on her solo transatlantic flight

She's all for the gals standing on their hind feet and doing their stuff for and by themselves. That's almost a fetish with her. But in her heart she wants independence all around—even for the masculine member of the team![64]

December 1932, *Pictorial Review*

> I'd rather have a baby.[65]

January 11, 1935; uttered as Earhart took off on her flight from Hawaii to California. Various news outlets took this to mean that he wanted her to have a child. He meant he preferred the pain of childbirth to worrying about her.

> No your honor. I'm just a relative and I disown her.[66]

Circa July 1937; George's flippant response to, "Are you responsible for this woman?" when Earhart was stopped for speeding in Blackwell, Oklahoma. The judge was not amused.

> I am deeply in love with you. . . . I'll be so happy when this is over. I want peace—and you. I'm never really content anymore when I'm away from you. So face the horrid likelihood of being held mighty close to me the rest of your days! Please love me a lot.[67]

Circa 1937

> I wish this flight wasn't hanging over us. You know I agree . . . with your ambition & will abet it. And 98 percent I know you'll get away with it. But we both recognize the hazards—and I love you dearly—and I don't want you to run risks.[68]

Circa 1937; reflecting on Earhart's impending round-the-world flight

> All I knew was that Amelia was more fun to play with than anyone else—I admired her ability, stood in awe of her information and intelligence, adored her imagination, and loved her for herself—and it held true always.[69]

Circa 1939

Amelia Earhart knew me better, probably, than anyone else ever can. With her discernment, why she married the man she did was often a matter of wonder to me. And to some others.[70]

Circa 1942

Amelia Earhart possessed those qualities of which, I think, hero-stuff is made.[71]

Circa 1942

Will Rogers (1879–1935), cowboy and commentator

Her personality equals her flying skill.[72]

April 19, 1935, *Plain Dealer* (Cleveland, OH)

She would be great in any business, or no business at all. She captivates the women too, which is unusual. . . . She has sure got the nerve, that gal.[73]

August 4, 1935, *Montana Standard* (Butte)

The thing I like about her is that she always has a fine word to say about all other aviators.[74]

August 4, 1935, *Omaha World Herald*

Eleanor Roosevelt (1884–1962), First Lady

She has done so many things which I have always wanted to do.[75]

Circa November 1932

She helped the case of women, by giving them a feeling there was nothing they could not do.[76]

Date unknown

Franklin Delano Roosevelt (1862–1945), president

From the days of these pioneers to the present era, women have marched step in step with men. And now, when air trails between our shores and those of our neighbors are being charted, you, as a woman, have preserved and carried forth this precious tradition.[77]

January 18, 1935; letter to Earhart

You have shown even the doubting Thomases that aviation is a science which can not be limited to men only.[78]

January 20, 1935, *Dallas Morning News*

Elinor Smith (1911–2010), pilot

To take Amelia's place as number-one woman pilot.[79]

Circa late 1928. When Smith expressed her ambition to George Putnam, he made it difficult for her to get sponsorships and publicity.

Maybe Amelia would have been a natural had she had the proper instruction and the amount of practice that went into it, but she never seemed to practice, to really stick at it.[80]

Date unknown

The image of a shy and retiring individual thrust against her will into the public eye was a figment of Putnam's lively imagination. Amelia was about as shy as Muhammad Ali.[81]

Circa 1981

Brynjulf Strandenaes (1871–?), Norwegian artist

She looks more like Lindbergh than Lindbergh himself.[82]

June 5, 1928, *Pittsburgh Press*

Louise Thaden (1905–1979), pilot

She wasn't especially good looking. . . . When she talked a warm personality overshadowed everything else, and she became, somehow, beautiful.[83]

Circa 1937

You've gone crazy on me. Why stick your neck out a mile on this round-the-world flight? You don't need to do anything more. You're tops now and if you *never* do anything you will always be. It seems to me you have everything to lose and nothing to gain. If you fall in the drink all you have accomplished during the last nine years will be lost.[84]

Circa 1937; Thaden's attempt to convince Earhart to abandon her round-the-world flight

I know she would have preferred to go out doing the thing she most wanted to do.[85]

July 9, 1937, *Richmond (VA) Times Dispatch*

Tide and Time, **British feminist magazine**

It would seem as if the public were infinitely more thrilled by the spectacle of women as passengers than by women as pilots. . . . When Lady Bailey and Lady Heath set out on their respective journeys there was a general feeling that women should not be allowed to take such risks. . . . But when Miss Earhart is carried, as a bundle might be carried, across the Atlantic, the press of two great countries echoes and re-echoes in excitement and President Coolidge himself sends his congratulations.[86]

Circa June 1928. Being described as nothing more than a bundle helped spur Earhart on to her 1932 solo crossing. The editor of the magazine was Lady Mary Bailey, a British aviator.

Walter Trumble (1879–1961), writer

Probably never again can Amelia Earhart walk on the streets of any city with the comfort of an ordinary citizen. She will be pushed and tugged and ever surrounded by the maddening throng.[87]

May 29, 1932, *Dallas Times Herald*; remark made after her solo transatlantic flight

Eugene Vidal (1895–1969), director of the Bureau of Air Commerce

She was an interesting person; a tomboy who liked all men's games, enjoyed being with mechanics working on airplanes, and yet was like a little girl. . . . Although often in trousers, she was very feminine and quite romantic in many ways.[88]

Unknown date

Gore Vidal (1925–2012), writer

I have walked the streets with many famous people in my time, from Greta Garbo to Paul Newman to Eleanor Roosevelt. No one got the crowd that Amelia got. She was—I must say it was beyond stardom. It was a strange continuum that she and Lindbergh occupied. They were like gods from outer space.[89]

Date unknown

Lillian Wald (1867–1940), social reformer

You represent the spirit of the settlements—always ready for a great adventure.[90]

July 9, 1928, *New York Times*

William Allen White (1868–1944), newspaper editor

Comb your head, kid, comb your head![91]

Circa 1937, *San Francisco Chronicle*. White, a family friend, teased Earhart about her unkempt hair.

Major Al Williams, (1896–1958), pilot and aircraft developer

Amelia Earhart's "Flying Laboratory" is the latest and most distressing racket that has been given to a trusting and enthusiastic public. . . . fat lecture contracts, the magazine and book rights . . . it's high time that [they] put an end to aviation's biggest racket—"Purely Scientific" ballyhoo.[92]

March 31, 1937, *Cleveland Press*. Earhart's response: "I'm glad it wasn't a woman who wrote it."

Notes

Chapter 1

1. Morrissey and Osborne, 16.
2. "Urges Women Take Up Flying," *Boston Daily Globe*, June 26, 1927. Similar quote: Earhart, "Try Flying Yourself," *Hearst's International-Cosmopolitan*, November 1928, 32.
3. Ware, 63.
4. "Amelia Earhart Spends Day Here; Gale Halts Ship," *Omaha World Herald*, October 10, 1928.
5. Earhart, *20 Hrs., 40 Min.*, 25.
6. Ibid., 47.
7. Ibid., 180.
8. Sue McNamara, "Noted Aviatrix Says Women Will Not Carry Mail," *San Diego Union*, March 3, 1929.
9. Earhart, "Shall You Let Your Daughter Fly?" *Hearst's International-Cosmopolitan*, March 1929, 89.
10. Earhart, "Fly America First," *Hearst's International-Cosmopolitan*, October 1929, 135.
11. Earhart, "Mother Reads as We Fly," *Hearst's International-Cosmopolitan*, January 1931, 17.

12. "Flying Doesn't Thrill Amelia—It's Scenery," *Milwaukee Journal*, October 29, 1932.
13. Janet Mabie, "A Bird's-Eye View of Fashions," *Christian Science Monitor*, February 7, 1934. See also Putnam, *Soaring Wings*, 205.
14. Florence Taaffe, "Miss Earhart, Famed Flier, Arrives in City—by Train," *Minneapolis Tribune*, December 1, 1934.
15. Janet Mabie, "Flivver Planes Flying Soon," unknown publication, circa 1934–1935, Earhart scrapbook 14, George Putnam Collection of Amelia Earhart Papers, Archives and Special Collections, Purdue University Library, West Lafayette, IN; hereafter GPPC.
16. "Two Ocean Hops Traced," *Los Angeles Times*, March 31, 1935. Similar quotes: Grace Farrington Gray, "We're Off," *The Farmer's Wife*, August 1935, 6; Earhart, "Miss Earhart's Own Story of Flight," *Los Angeles Times*, January 13, 1935.
17. Earhart, *Last Flight*, 13.
18. Putnam, *Soaring Wings*, 67. Similar quote: Earhart, "My Flight from Hawaii," *National Geographic*, May 1935, 605.
19. "Amelia Earhart Declares Aviators Are Not Thrill Seekers, " *Huntington (IN) Herald Press*, undated clipping, GPPC, b9f297i7.
20. "Flying Doesn't Thrill Amelia—It's Scenery," *Milwaukee Journal*, October 29, 1932.
21. R. Gibson Hubbard, "Scribe Learns Miss Earhart Is Very Feminine," *Oregon Journal* (Portland), February 1, 1933.
22. Earhart, *20 Hrs., 40 Min.*, 25.
23. Ware, 73.
24. Earhart, *The Fun of It*, 167.
25. Ibid., 179.
26. "Take to the Air," *Boston Herald*, July 3, 1927.
27. Earhart, *20 Hrs., 40 Min.*, 20.
28. "Thrill of Flying Gone Amelia Declares," *Milwaukee Sentinel*, October 29, 1932.
29. Janet Mabie, "Flivver Planes Flying Soon," unknown publication, circa 1934–1935, Earhart scrapbook 14, GPPC.

30. "Aviatrix Arrives after 'Longest Ride on Train,'" *Minneapolis Star*, March 30, 1935.
31. "12 Women Get Honor Degrees at Oglethorpe," unknown newspaper, circa May 26, 1935, Earhart scrapbook 14, GPPC.
32. Nellie Webb, "Amelia More Than on Time," *Atchison (KS) Daily Globe*, June 7, 1935.
33. Butler, 343; Winters, 168. Similar quote: "for a shiny new one to shake down," *Brockton (MA) Daily Enterprise*, December 11, 1935.
34. Earhart and Backus, 202.
35. Putnam, *Soaring Wings*, 275.
36. Earhart, *Last Flight*, 11.
37. Ibid., 25.
38. Ibid.
39. Ibid., 47.
40. "Amelia Earhart Flies 'Windmill' Airplane to Unofficial Altitude Record of 19,000 Feet in East," *San Diego Union*, April 9, 1931.
41. "Woman Flyer Again Wins Distinction," *Los Angeles Times*, June 8, 1931. Similar quote: "Mrs. Putnam Lauds New Type of Airship," *Riverside (CA) Daily Press*, June 8, 1931.
42. Earhart, "A Friendly Flight Across," *New York Times*, July 19, 1931.
43. Earhart, "Your Next Garage May House an Autogiro," *Hearst's International-Cosmopolitan*, August 1931, 58.
44. "Too Busy with Lectures to Make Plans for New Flights," *Zanesville (OH) Signal*, December 1, 1935.
45. "Amelia Earhart's Big Leap," unknown magazine, possibly *American*, circa May 1935, Earhart scrapbook 14, GPPC. Similar quote: "It's more fun than any roller coaster I ever rode," Putnam, *Soaring Wings*, 219.
46. Putnam, *Soaring Wings*, 219.
47. Earhart, "Here Is How Fannie Hurst Could Learn to Fly," *Hearst's International-Cosmopolitan*, January 1929, 37.
48. From an unpublished manuscript by Janet Mabie, Butler, 278. Similar quote: "City Giving Joyous Acclaim to Woman Who Flew across Atlantic Alone," *New York Herald Tribune*, June 21, 1932.

49. Lindsey H. Spight, "Amelia Earhart Makes Charming Talk to Advertising Club," unnamed publication, circa 1930s, Earhart scrapbook 2, GPPC.
50. Earhart, *The Fun of It*, 39.
51. Ibid., 162.
52. Earhart, "Amelia Earhart Delays Take-Off," *Boston Daily Globe*, May 2, 1935.
53. Earhart, "My Flight from Hawaii," *National Geographic*, May 1935, 605.
54. Earhart, *Last Flight*, 1.
55. Putnam, *Soaring Wings*, 87.
56. "Miss Earhart on Her Adventure," *Times* (London), June 21, 1928. Quote also appeared in American newspapers.
57. Earhart, "Miss Earhart Says 'Flying Clothes' Are Unnecessary for Women," *New York Times*, June 22, 1928.
58. Ibid.
59. "New York Hails Amelia Earhart as 'Lady Lindy,'" *Christian Science Monitor*, July 6, 1928.
60. Lovell, 129.
61. "Women Fliers Balk at Easy $10,000 Race," *New York Times*, June 12, 1929.
62. "Women Are Held Back, Miss Earhart Finds," *New York Times*, July 30, 1929.
63. Earhart, "Why Are Women Afraid to Fly," *Hearst's International-Cosmopolitan*, July 1929, 138.
64. Ibid.
65. "How Women Take to the Air," *Literary Digest*, October 26, 1929, 56.
66. Ibid.
67. Florence Yoder Wilson, "What Women Can Do for Aviation," *Needlecraft: The Magazine of Home Arts*, May 1930, 16.
68. "Inbred Timidity Handicap to Women, Says Amelia Earhart," *Seattle Daily Times*, July 15, 1930.
69. "Miss Earhart Raps Flying Feminists," *Boston Daily Globe*, August 14, 1930.
70. "Women in Aviation Held Equal to Men," *New York Times*, May 9, 1931.
71. "Women Score Lead in New Air Marks," *San Diego Union*, July 26, 1931.

72. Ware, 80.
73. "Amelia Earhart Reaches London," *Florence (AL) Times*, May 24, 1932.
74. "Miss Earhart Flew for Sex," *Boston Daily Globe*, May 24, 1932.
75. "Give Women Equality, Urges Amelia Earhart," *Spokane (WA) Daily Chronicle*, September 23, 1932.
76. "Amelia Given Thiel Degree," *McKeesport (PA) Daily News*, December 15, 1932.
77. "Amelia Earhart Putnam Discusses Women in the Field of Aviation," *The Campus* (Sarah Lawrence College), January 23, 1933. Similar quotes: "How Women Take to the Air," *Literary Digest*, October 26, 1929, 56; "Miss Earhart Raps Flying Feminists," *Boston Daily Globe*, August 14, 1930.
78. "Amelia Earhart Is Most Modest about Her Flights," *Vancouver (BC) Daily Province*, February 4, 1933.
79. "In Air Race So Her Sex Can Profit," *New York Telegram*, June 30, 1933.
80. "Amelia Wants Equality for Women Aviators," *Boston Daily Globe*, September 26, 1933. Similar quote: Earhart, *The Fun of It*, 152.
81. "Cake-Baking Boast of Amelia Earhart Who Flew Atlantic," *Times Union* (Albany, NY), November 22, 1933.
82. Earhart, *The Fun of It*, 95.
83. Ibid., 148–49.
84. Rich 100–101.
85. Butler, 304.
86. "Air Successes Open New Fields to Women," *Los Angeles Times*, September 8, 1936.
87. Thaden, 148.
88. Ibid., 148–49.
89. Putnam, *Soaring Wings*, 84.

Chapter 2

1. Earhart, "Flying the Atlantic—and Selling Sausages Have a Lot of Things in Common," *American Magazine*, August 1932, 72.
2. "All Must Fly Sooner or Later, Amelia Earhart, Who Is Rabid Air Fan,

Tells 400 Clubwomen," *Dallas Morning News*, December 7, 1933. Similar quote: Earhart, *The Fun of It*, 25.

3. "Amelia Earhart Expects to Take Off This Morning. Thea Rasches Plane Delivered," *Washington Post*, June 8, 1928.
4. "Air Heroine Resting Up," *Rochester (NY) Evening Journal*, June 18, 1928.
5. "Miss Earhart Too Excited to Relieve Pilot on Flight, *Morning Star* (Rockford, IL), June 19, 1928.
6. "Future of Ocean Flights," *Times* (London), June 20, 1928.
7. "Miss Earhart Spurns Fashion," *New York Sun*, June 20, 1928.
8. Earhart, "Miss Earhart Learning What It Is to Be Famous," *Boston Herald*, June 21, 1928. Similar quotes: "Home City Gives Amelia Earhart Great Welcome," *Christian Science Monitor*, July 10, 1928; "Aviatrix Appears in Borrowed Clothes," *Rochester (NY) Evening Journal*, June 20, 1928; Earhart, *The Fun of It*, 84.
9. "New York Hails Amelia Earhart as 'Lady Lindy,'" *Christian Science Monitor*, July 6, 1928.
10. "Lindberg Girl Wins Manhattan," *Cleveland Plain Dealer*, July 7, 1928.
11. Ibid.
12. "Amelia a 'Social Worker on a Bat,'" *Cleveland Plain Dealer*, July 8, 1928.
13. "Thrill Lacking in Ocean Flight," *Los Angeles Times*, July 12, 1928. Similar quote: Miss Earhart Too Excited to Relieve Pilot on Flight, *Morning Star* (Rockford, IL), June 19, 1928.
14. "I was really only baggage" in "The Heroine of Friendship," *Outlook*, July 1928, 449.
15. Earhart, "Dropping in on England," *McCall's*, October 1928, 21.
16. Earhart, *20 Hrs., 40 Min.*, 39.
17. Ibid., 40.
18. Ibid., 42.
19. Earhart, *The Fun of It*, 84. Similar quote: "Miss Earhart and Partner Take Private Car to New York," *Boston Herald*, July 11, 1928.
20. Lovell, 129.

21. Ware, 43.
22. Ferris, 7.
23. "Miss Earhart Visions Age When All Will Fly," *Morning Star* (Rockford, IL), October 25, 1933.
24. "Don't Want Men's Aid in Flying Over Rockies," *New York Times*, June 12, 1929.
25. Thaden, 51.
26. Putnam, *Soaring Wings*, 99.
27. Ibid., 110.
28. "First Woman Spans Ocean in Solo Trip," *Christian Science Monitor*, May 21, 1932.
29. Untitled article, *The American*, May 22, 1932, Earhart scrapbook 7, GPPC, AESB007.
30. "Mrs. Putnam Says Husband Proved Good Sport in Consenting to Flight," *Boston Herald*, May 22, 1932.
31. "Miss Earhart's Own Story," *Northern Whig and Belfast Post*, May 23, 1932. Similar quote: Linton Wells, "Amelia Earhart Flies to England in Storm," unidentified British newspaper, May 22, 1932, Amelia Earhart Papers, Schlesinger Library, Radcliffe Institute, Harvard University, Cambridge, MA (hereafter SLRC), A-129, series V, 69.
32. "Amelia Meets Her Husband in France," *Telegraph* (Nashua, NH), June 3, 1932.
33. Putnam, *Soaring Wings*, 127. Similar quotes: "Geographic Society Honors Mrs. Putnam," *New York Times*, June 22, 1932; "City Giving Joyous Acclaim to Woman Who Flew across Atlantic Alone," *New York Herald Tribune*, June 21, 1932; "The Society's Special Medal Awarded to Amelia Earhart," *National Geographic*, September 1932, 367.
34. "City Giving Joyous Acclaim to Woman Who Flew across Atlantic Alone," *New York Herald Tribune*, June 21, 1932. Similar quote: "The Society's Special Medal Awarded to Amelia Earhart," *National Geographic*, September 1932, 367.
35. "The Society's Special Medal Awarded to Amelia Earhart," *National Geographic*, September 1932, 363.

36. "Amelia Earhart Putnam Guest of Her Early Flying Associates," *Boston Daily Globe*, June 30, 1932.
37. Earhart, "Flying the Atlantic—and Selling Sausages Have a Lot of Things in Common," *American Magazine*, August 1932, 72.
38. Ibid.
39. Earhart, "Women and Courage," *Hearst's International-Cosmopolitan*, September 1932, 147.
40. "The Society's Special Medal Awarded to Amelia Earhart," *National Geographic*, September 1932, 367.
41. Putnam, *Soaring Wings*, 108.
42. "Amelia Earhart 'Flies Atlantic' Again to Tune of Many Questions," *Omaha World Herald*, December 12, 1933. Similar quote: Richard E. Gnade, "First Lady of Air Relates Adventures during Pacific Hop," *Chautauqua (NY) Daily*, August 10, 1935.
43. "Amelia Crosses Nation Nonstop," *Boston Daily Globe*, August 26, 1932.
44. "In Air Race So Her Sex Can Profit," *New York Telegram*, June 30, 1933.
45. Arthur Brisbane, "Today," *Rochester (NY) Journal*, August 31, 1935.
46. Letter from Earhart to Amy Otis Earhart, circa September 4, 1935, SLRC, MC 398, Series I 16.
47. Putnam, *Soaring Wings*, 255.
48. "Earhart to Sail Tonight," *Los Angeles Times*, December 22, 1934.
49. Letter from Earhart to George Putnam, January 8, 1935, GPPC, b4f40i1.
50. Letter from Earhart to Earnest C. Clark, January 10, 1935, GPPC, b4f40i4.
51. Earhart, "Amelia Earhart's Own Story of Her Flight over Pacific," *New York Times*, January 13, 1935. Similar quote: Putnam, *Soaring Wings*, 254.
52. Earhart, "Amelia Earhart's Own Story of Her Flight over Pacific," *New York Times*, January 13, 1935.
53. Ibid.
54. Burke, 147.

55. Earhart, "My Flight from Hawaii," *National Geographic*, May 1935, 596.
56. Ibid., 605.
57. Richard E. Gnade, "First Lady of Air Relates Adventures during Pacific Hop," *Chautauqua (NY) Daily*, August 10, 1935.
58. "Bug Breaks Flight of Miss Earhart," *New York Times*, May 9, 1935.
59. "Miss Earhart Sets Mark in 2,100-Mile Air Dash from Mexico to Newark," *New York Times*, May 9, 1935.
60. Putnam, *Soaring Wings*, 265.
61. Earhart, *Last Flight*, 10.
62. Putnam, *Soaring Wings*, 245.
63. Letter from Earhart to Amy Otis Earhart, April 1, 1936, SLRC, MC 398, Series I 17. Similar quote: Putnam, *Soaring Wings*, 273.
64. "Amelia Earhart Prepares to Fly Round the World," *Christian Science Monitor*, February 12, 1937.
65. James Bassett Jr., "Amelia Earhart Back in City," *Los Angeles Times*, March 7, 1937.
66. "Aviatrix Earhart Ready for Globe Girdling Hop," *San Francisco Chronicle*, March 12, 1937.
67. "Earhart Plane Is Described by Her as Standard Machine," *Christian Science Monitor*, March 18, 1937.
68. Ibid.
69. "The Flight Will Go On," *Christian Science Monitor*, March 20, 1937.
70. Earhart, *Last Flight*, 41.
71. Winters, 198.
72. "Amelia to Try Long Hop Again," *Boston Daily Globe*, April 12, 1937.
73. "Earhart Take-Off from Miami Soon," *New York Times*, May 30, 1937.
74. Letter from Earhart to Amy Otis Earhart, circa May 1937, SLRC, MC 398, Series I 18.
75. Lovell, 262.
76. "Amelia Set for 'Worst,'" *Portsmouth (OH) Times*, June 28, 1937. Similar quote: "Miss Earhart Flies for New Guinea Field," *New York Times*, June 29, 1937.
77. Earhart, *Last Flight*, 76.

78. Lovell, 259; Earhart, *Last Flight*, 76.
79. Earhart, *Last Flight*, 105.
80. Ibid., 133.
81. Lovell, 282. See also letter to Captain Joseph Gervais from the law firm of Baird & Holley in Los Angeles, October 24, 1962, SLRC, A-24, Series IV, 53.
82. Earhart, *Last Flight*, 128.
83. Thaden, 150.
84. Earhart, *Last Flight*, 30. Similar quote: "Because I wanted to make it. Shining adventure offers new experiences and added knowledge of flying and of peoples and of myself," Putnam, *Soaring Wings*, 254.
85. Letter from Earhart to George Palmer Putnam; Earhart, *Last Flight*, 134. Also in Putnam, *Soaring Wings*, 46.
86. Earhart, *Last Flight*, xvi.
87. Ibid., 39.
88. Ibid., 44.
89. Ibid., 61.
90. Putnam, *Soaring Wings*, 208.
91. "Amelia Escapes Sans Injury," *Evening Tribune* (San Diego, CA), June 12, 1931.
92. Letter from Earhart to Amy Otis Earhart, circa July 1931, SLRC, MC 398, Series I 13.
93. Letter from Earhart to Amy Otis Earhart, September 17, 1931, SLRC, MC 398, Series I 13. See also "Amelia Earhart Crashes Again," *Boston Herald*, September 13, 1931.
94. Putnam, *Soaring Wings*, 210.
95. Nichols, 209.
96. "Amelia Earhart Back in City," *Los Angeles Times*, Marcg 26, 1937.
97. "Ride in Traffic Police Car Thrills Miss Earhart," *Boston Daily Globe*, July 8, 1928.
98. Letter from Earhart to Amy Otis Earhart, November 22, 1929, SLRC, MC 398, Series I 11.
99. "Miss Earhart Sets Autogiro Record" *New York Times*, April 9, 1931.
100. Earhart, *The Fun of It*, 161.

Chapter 3

1. Earhart, "Miss Earhart Foresees Planes de Luxe, Due to Women's Interest in Aviation," *New York Times*, June 20, 1928.
2. Earhart, "Shall You Let Your Daughter Fly?" *Hearst's International-Cosmopolitan*, March 1929, 143.
3. "Earhart Suggests New Note for Aviation Advertising," Chicago newspaper, May 20, 1930, Earhart scrapbook 2, GPPC.
4. Earhart, "Mother Reads as We Fly," *Hearst's International-Cosmopolitan*, January 1931, 17.
5. "Miss Earhart Rates Planes Safe as Autos," *New York Times*, March 8, 1931. Similar quote: Earhart, "Shall You Let Your Daughter Fly?" *Hearst's International-Cosmopolitan*, March 1929, 88.
6. "Amelia Earhart, Famous Aviatrix, Urges Aviation for College Men before Williamstown Broadcast," *Williams Record* (Williams College), November 15, 1932.
7. "Amelia Earhart Putnam Discusses Women in the Field of Aviation," *The Campus* (Sarah Lawrence College), January 23, 1933.
8. "Women Fliers to Help in Next War Miss Earhart Says; North Pole Lures," *Oregonian* (Portland), February 2, 1933.
9. Mortimer Franklin, "Amelia Earhart Looks at the Films!" *Screenland*, June 1933, 29.
10. Gilroy, 19.
11. Earhart, "Are American Women Holding Aviation Back," *Liberty*, February 13, 1937, 14.
12. Earhart, *Last Flight*, 30.
13. Lindsey H. Spight, "Amelia Earhart Makes Charming Talk to Advertising Club," unnamed publication, circa 1930s, Earhart scrapbook 2, GPPC.
14. Ibid.
15. Putnam, *Soaring Wings*, 251.
16. "Ride in Traffic Police Car Thrills Miss Earhart," *Boston Daily Globe*, July 8, 1928. Similar quote: Earhart, *20 Hrs., 40 Min.*, 123.
17. "U.S. Leads World in Flying, Amelia Earhart Tells Erie," *Erie (PA) Daily Times*, December 1, 1932.

18. Earhart, *20 Hrs., 40 Min.*, 123–24.
19. "Permanent Air Mail Bill Urged by Amelia," *Register-Republican* (Rockford, IL), March 20, 1934.
20. Earhart, "Fly America First," *Hearst's International-Cosmopolitan*, October 1929, 136.
21. Ibid.
22. Earhart, "Your Next Garage May House an Autogiro," *Hearst's International-Cosmopolitan*, August 1931, 58.
23. "Ocean Air Lines Inevitable, Says Mrs. Putnam," *Christian Science Monitor*, June 8, 1932.
24. "Amelia Plans New Flight over Ocean," *Boston Daily Globe*, June 25, 1932. Similar quotes: "Miss Earhart Returns Here," *Los Angeles Times*, July 4, 1932; "Washington Receives and Honors Aviatrix," *Greensboro (NC) Daily News*, June 22, 1932; Manthei Howe, "Trans-Atlantic Flying Common Thing Soon, Famed Aviatrix in Talk," *Daily Mining Journal* (Marquette, MI), October 25, 1932; "Forsees Air Service over Sea in 2 Years," *Toronto Daily Star*, December 14, 1932.
25. Earhart, "The Future of Aviation," *Cosmopolitan*, February 1933, 126.
26. Ibid.
27. Earhart, *The Fun of It*, 167.
28. Janet Mabie, "Flivver Planes Flying Soon," unknown publication, circa 1934–1935, Earhart scrapbook 14, GPPC.
29. "Amelia Earhart, Conqueror of Pacific, Talks Transportation with Akron Women," *Akron (OH) Beacon*, February 14, 1935.
30. "Amelia Earhart Says Cheap Airplanes Are Near," *Boston Daily Globe*, March 7, 1935.
31. "A Woman in the News," *Christian Science Monitor*, January 16, 1936.
32. "Amelia Earhart Prepares to Fly Round the World," *Christian Science Monitor*, February 12, 1937.
33. "Women Urged to Fly," unknown newspaper, circa 1935, Earhart scrapbook 14, GPPC.

Chapter 4

1. Earhart, *20 Hrs., 40 Min.*, 103.
2. Earhart, *The Fun of It*, 208.
3. Ibid.
4. Ware, 79.
5. "Amelia Earhart Prepares to Fly Round the World," *Christian Science Monitor*, February 12, 1937.
6. "Amelia Tells of Hawaii Hop," *Boston Daily Globe*, March 19, 1937.
7. Putnam, *Soaring Wings*, 156.
8. "New Essex Line Makes Its Debut," *Detroit Free Press*, July 22, 1932.
9. Letter from Earhart to Amy Otis Earhart, September 18, 1932, SLRC, MC 398, Series I 14.
10. "Amelia Earhart Here Says Cheap Airplanes Are Near," March 7, 1935, unknown Boston newspaper, Earhart scrapbook 14, GPPC, AESB014.
11. Putnam, *Soaring Wings*, 140.
12. "Miss Earhart Speaks Tonight," *Boston Herald*, November 14, 1928. Similar quote: Earhart and Backus, 135.
13. Earhart, *The Fun of It*, 207–8.
14. "Amelia Earhart, Conqueror of Pacific, Talks Transportation with Akron Women," *Akron (OH) Beacon*, February 14, 1935.
15. "Amelia Earhart Here to Lecture on Recent Flight," *Kansas City (KS) Journal*, February 18, 1935.
16. "Aviatrix Arrives after 'Longest Ride on Train,'" *Minneapolis Star*, March 30, 1935.
17. Earhart, "The Future of Aviation," *Hearst's International-Cosmopolitan*, February 1933, 126.
18. Ibid.
19. Ibid.
20. Ibid.

Chapter 5

1. Earhart, *20 Hrs., 40 Min.*, 166.
2. Putnam, *Soaring Wings*, 249.
3. "Home as Well as Sky Is Amelia's Heaven," unnamed Omaha newspaper, February 19, 1935, Earhart scrapbook 14, GPPC, AESB014.
4. "Miss Earhart Spurns Fashion," *New York Sun*, June 20, 1928.
5. Earhart, "Flying the Atlantic—and Selling Sausages Have a Lot of Things in Common," *American Magazine*, August 1932, 72.
6. Earhart, "My Husband," *Redbook*, September 1932, 97.
7. "A Camera Interview with Amelia Earhart," *Cleveland* [illegible] *Review*, December 4 or 14, 1932, Earhart scrapbook 8, GPPC, AESB008.
8. Earhart, "Amelia Earhart on the Minimum Wage Law," unnamed newspaper, March 7, 1933, Earhart scrapbook 10, GPPC, AESB010.
9. Earhart, *The Fun of It*, 26.
10. Ware, 92; Rich, 155.
11. "Earn Own Living, Miss Earhart Tells Women," *Columbus (OH) Citizen*, January 12, 1934.
12. "Amelia Comes to Town—But by Train This Time," *Minneapolis Journal*, March 30, 1935.
13. Earhart, "Amelia Earhart Delays Take-Off," *Boston Daily Globe*, May 2, 1935.
14. Butler, 336. Similar quote: "Earhart: Good-will Emissary Again Achieves the Unusual," *Newsweek*, May 18, 1935, 35.
15. Marguerite Martyn, unknown title, *Post Dispatch* (St. Louis), April 7, 1936, SLRC, A-129-15. Similar quote: Putnam, *Soaring Wings*, 140.
16. Putnam, *Soaring Wings*, 251.
17. Letter from Earhart to Amy Otis Earhart, August 26, 1928, SLRC, MC 398, Series I 11.
18. Letter from Earhart to Amy Otis Earhart, April 1931, SLRC, MC 398, Series I 13.
19. Letter from Earhart to Amy Otis Earhart, circa autumn 1931, SLRC,

MC 398, Series I 13. Similar quote: Letter from Earhart to Amy Otis Earhart, October 12, 1930, SLRC, MC 398, Series I 12.
20. Letter from Earhart to Amy Otis Earhart, February 13, 1933, SLRC, MC 398, Series I 15.
21. Earhart and Backus, 176.
22. Putnam, *Soaring Wings*, 141.

Chapter 6

1. Earhart, "Are You Air-Minded, *Independent Woman*, October 1933, 359.
2. "Amelia Turns 'Career Pilot,'" *Ogden (UT) Standard-Examiner*, May 17, 1936.
3. Putnam, *Soaring Wings*, 248–49.
4. Ibid., 249.
5. Ibid.
6. Ibid.
7. Ware, 40.
8. Putnam, *Soaring Wings*, 49.
9. Ibid.
10. Ibid., 50.
11. Lovell, 128.
12. "Women Score Lead in New Air Marks," *San Diego Union*, July 26, 1931.
13. "So They Say," *Golden Book Magazine*, July 1931, 39.
14. "Amelia Earhart Is Visitor to Va. Air Derby," *Richmond (VA) Times Dispatch*, September 25, 1932.
15. Earhart, "My Husband," *Redbook*, September 1932, 97.
16. Putnam, *Soaring Wings*, 86.
17. Earhart, "Flying the Atlantic—and Selling Sausages Have a Lot of Things in Common," *American Magazine*, August 1932, 17.
18. Amelia Earhart Flies to the Defense of Her Sex as a 'Disgusted Male' Cries: Women Are a Total Flop Outside the Home," *Plain Dealer* (Cleveland, OH), June 3, 1934.

19. "Aviatrix Arrives after 'Longest Ride on Train,'" *Minneapolis Star*, March 30, 1935. Similar quote: Putnam, *Soaring Wings*, 250.
20. "Two Ocean Hops Traced," *Los Angeles Times*, March 31, 1935.
21. Butler, 311.
22. "Amelia Turns 'Career Pilot,'" *Seattle Daily Times*, May 17, 1936.
23. Ibid.
24. Putnam, *Soaring Wings*, 90.
25. Ibid., 141.
26. Ibid.
27. Ibid., 144.
28. "Favorite Recipes of Famous Women," *Times-Picayune* (New Orleans, LA), February 6, 1932. Similar quote: "Amelia Earhart Putnam Discusses Women in the Field of Aviation," *The Campus* (Sarah Lawrence College, Bronxville, NY), January 23, 1933.
29. "Amelia Earhart Brings Message to Wives; Urges Gainful Work," *Seattle Post-Intelligencer*, February 4, 1933.
30. "Miss Earhart Sees Women Changing," *Journal American* (New York, NY), November 23, 1933.
31. Putnam, *Soaring Wings*, 139.
32. Ibid., 147.
33. "Amelia Proves Self Modest and Genial," *Boston Daily Globe*, January 13, 1935. The *New York Times*, January 13, 1935, recorded her saying, "Not while there's life in the old horse left."
34. "Amelia Earhart Resting; Trying to 'Be Herself,'" *Dayton Daily News*, August 25, 1935.
35. Putnam, *Soaring Wings*, 86.

Chapter 7

1. Putnam, *Soaring Wings*, 153.
2. Ibid., 116; Putnam, "The Forgotten Husband," *Pictorial Review*, December 1932.

3. "Unified Control of Transport," *Christian Science Monitor*, March 16, 1934.
4. "Mrs. Davie New Deal War Is Assailed by Miss Earhart," unnamed paper, undated, Earhart scrapbook 14, GPPC, AESB014. Similar quote: "Feminine Leaders Offer Reasons for Thanksgiving Day Gratitude," *Repository* (Canton, OH), December 1, 1933.
5. "Amelia Earhart, Conqueror of Pacific, Talks Transportation with Akron Women," *Akron (OH) Beacon*, February 14, 1935.
6. Letter from Earhart to Amy Otis Earhart, circa May 1936, SLRC, MC 398, Series I 17.
7. Telegram from Earhart to Eleanor Roosevelt, September 15, 1936, FDRL, http://www.fdrlibrary.marist.edu/_resources/images/ersel/erse1034.pdf#search=earhart.
8. "Earhart for Roosevelt," *New York Times*, September 20, 1936.
9. Lovell, 31.
10. Putnam, *Soaring Wings*, 152.

Chapter 8

1. Earhart, *20 Hrs., 40 Min*, 3.
2. Earhart, *The Fun of It*, 19.
3. Earhart, *20 Hrs., 40 Min.*, 5.
4. Earhart, "Shall You Let Your Daughter Fly?" *Hearst's International-Cosmopolitan*, March 1929, 142.
5. "Women Fliers to Help in Next War, Miss Earhart Says; North Pole Lures," *Morning Oregonian* (Portland), February 2, 1933.
6. Ibid.
7. "Amelia Earhart Is Most Modest about Her Flights," *Vancouver (BC) Daily Province*, February 4, 1933.
8. "Draft Women for War Says Miss Earhart," unnamed Los Angeles newspaper, February 5, 1933, GPPC, AESB010.
9. Ibid. Similar quote: "Would Laugh War Out of Existence," *Omaha World Herald*, citing the *New York World-Telegram*, November 11, 1933.

10. "Draft Women for War Says Miss Earhart," unnamed Los Angeles newspaper, February 5, 1933, GPPC, AESB010.
11. Daughters of the American Revolution, 655.
12. Mortimer Franklin, "Amelia Earhart Looks at the Films!" *Screenland*, June 1933, 29.
13. "'Let Old Men Fight,' Amelia Earhart Urges," *New York Times*, November 11, 1933.
14. W. J. Taylor, "Noted Aviatrix Would Man Bomber," unknown newspaper, undated but likely 1933–1934, Earhart scrapbook 3, GPPC, AESB003. Similar quotes: "Draft Women for War," *Home Magazine*, August 1935, 23; untitled article, *Quest*, February 1936, Earhart scrapbook 14, GPPC, AESB014.
15. "Story Untrue, Denial of Amelia," *Evening Tribune* (San Diego), September 11, 1934.
16. "Draft Women for War," *The Home Magazine*, August 1935, 22.
17. Ibid., 25.
18. Ibid., 23.
19. Ibid., 25.
20. Ibid.
21. Putnam, *Soaring Wings*, 149.
22. Ibid.

Chapter 9

1. Letter from Earhart to Virginia Park, March 7, 1914, SLRC, MC 398, Series I, 7.
2. "Miss Earhart Gives Girls' Plane Trophy," *New York Times*, May 26, 1929. Similar quote: Earhart, *Last Flight*, 25.
3. "Inbred Timidity Handicap to Women, Says Amelia Earhart," *Seattle Daily Times*, July 15, 1930.
4. "Women in Aviation Held Equal to Men," *New York Times*, May 8, 1931.

5. Earhart, "Flying the Atlantic—and Selling Sausages Have a Lot of Things in Common," *American Magazine*, August 1932, 72.
6. Earhart, *The Fun of It*, 53.
7. Ibid., 143–44.
8. Putnam, *Soaring Wings*, 155.
9. "Amelia Earhart Is Helping Youth," unknown publication, circa 1934–1935, Earhart scrapbook 2, GPPC, AESB002.
10. Ibid.
11. "Amelia Earhart 'Just One of the Girls,' as Consultant at Purdue," *Indianapolis News*, November 27, 1935.
12. Ibid. Similar quote: "Amelia Earhart Is Helping Youth," unknown publication, circa 1934–1935, Earhart scrapbook 2, GPPC, AESB002.
13. Amelia Turns 'Career Pilot,'" *Seattle Daily Times*, May 17, 1936. Similar quote: "Flyer Urges Job Stability," *Los Angeles Times*, November 28, 1935.
14. Ibid.
15. Earhart, *Last Flight*, 26.
16. Winters, 80.
17. Earhart, *20 Hrs., 40 Min.*, 165.
18. Earhart, *The Fun of It*, 87.
19. Ibid., 6.
20. Ibid., 5.
21. Putnam, *Soaring Wings*, 88.
22. Ibid., 89.

Chapter 10

1. "Miss Earhart Flew for Sex," *Boston Daily Globe*, May 24, 1932.
2. "Amelia Earhart Is Visitor to Va. Air Derby," *Richmond (VA) Times Dispatch*, September 25, 1932.
3. Gordon Sinclair, "'I'm Not a Torch-Bearer' Amelia Earhart Declares," *Toronto Daily Star*, December 12, 1932.

4. "Amelia Earhart Is Most Modest about Her Flights," *Vancouver (BC) Daily Province*, February 4, 1933.
5. Earhart, *20 Hrs., 14 Min.*, 140.
6. "Amelia Earhart, Visitor Here, Discusses Work and Clothes," *Richmond (VA) Times Dispatch*, February 2, 1934.
7. Ibid. Similar quote: Earhart, *The Fun of It*, 145–46.
8. "Amelia Earhart Flies to the Defense of Her Sex as a 'Disgusted Male' Cries: Women Are a Total Flop Outside the Home," *Plain Dealer* (Cleveland, OH), June 3, 1934.
9. "Amelia Wins Acclaim Here," *Morning Star* (Rockford, IL), February 23, 1935.
10. Mary E. Bostwick, "Amelia Anticipates Busy Day at Races," likely Indianapolis newspaper, circa May 1935, Earhart scrapbook 14, GPPC.
11. Letter from Earhart to Dr. Raymond S. Holtz, October 7, 1935, b8f247i1, GPPC.
12. "Amelia Earhart Putnam Discusses Women in the Field of Aviation," *The Campus* (Sarah Lawrence College, Bronxville, NY), January 23, 1933.
13. "Earn Own Living, Miss Earhart Tells Women," *Columbus (OH) Citizen*, January 12, 1934.
14. "Amelia Earhart, Visitor Here, Discusses Work and Clothes," *Richmond (VA) Times Dispatch*, February 2, 1934.
15. "Amelia Earhart Busy Breaking Precedents; Now She Tries a Hand at Dress Designing," *Springfield (MA) Republican*, May 18, 1934.
16. "Amelia Earhart Flies to the Defense of Her Sex as a 'Disgusted Male' Cries: Women Are a Total Flop Outside the Home," *Plain Dealer* (Cleveland, OH), June 3, 1934.
17. Winters, 69.
18. "Amelia Earhart Flies to the Defense of Her Sex as a 'Disgusted Male' Cries: Women Are a Total Flop Outside the Home," *Plain Dealer* (Cleveland, OH), June 3, 1934.
19. Putnam, *Soaring Wings*, 173.
20. Ibid., 144.
21. Earhart, "Why Are Women Afraid to Fly," *Hearst's International-Cosmopolitan*, July 1929, 138.

22. Ibid.
23. Earhart, "The Feminine Touch, *Aero News and Mechanics*, April/May 1930, 35.
24. "Inbred Timidity Handicap to Women, Says Amelia Earhart," *Seattle Daily Times*, July 15, 1930. Similar quote: "Amelia Earhart Lovely Guest," *Spokesman-Review* (Spokane, WA), January 31, 1933.
25. "Amelia Earhart Buys Franklin," advertisement, *Times-Picayune* (New Orleans, LA), April 19, 1931.
26. Gordon Sinclair, "'I'm Not a Torch-Bearer' Amelia Earhart Declares," *Toronto Daily Star*, December 12, 1932.
27. Ibid.
28. "New Year's Resolutions of Notables of United States," *Aberdeen (SD) Daily News*, January 1, 1933.
29. Earhart, *The Fun of It*, 138.
30. Putnam, *Soaring Wings*, 46.
31. "Amelia Proves Self Modest and Genial," *Boston Daily Globe*, January 13, 1935.
32. "Famous Flyer Tells of Hop over Pacific," unknown Marion, Indiana, newspaper, February 22, 1935, Earhart scrapbook 14, GPPC.
33. Richard E. Gnade, "First Lady of Air Relates Adventures during Pacific Hop," *Chautauqua (NY) Daily*, August 10, 1935.
34. Letter from Earhart to Dr. Raymond S. Holtz, B8f247i1, GPPC.
35. Telegram from Earhart to Jo Berger, November 9, 1935, b4f45i1, GPPC.
36. "Amelia Earhart Back; Full of Ideas about Young Women," *New York World Telegram*, December 2, 1935.
37. Ibid.
38. Putnam, *Soaring Wings*, 89–90.
39. "Should a Wife Support Herself," unknown publication, undated, b9f297i3, GPPC.
40. "Amelia Earhart Buys Franklin," advertisement, *Times-Picayune* (New Orleans, LA), April 19, 1931.
41. "Women Are Held Back, Miss Earhart Finds," *New York Times*, July 30, 1929.
42. "President Hears Plea for Women's Rights," *New York Times*, September 23, 1932.

43. Ibid. Similar quote: Rich, 160.
44. "Unified Control of Transport," *Christian Science Monitor*, March 16, 1934.
45. "Draft Women for War," *The Home Magazine*, August 1935, 23. Similar quote: Putnam, *Soaring Wings*, 149.
46. *The American Experience: Amelia Earhart* (Boston, MA: PBS video, WGBH/Boston, Nancy Porter Productions, 1993).
47. Earhart, "Women and Courage," *Hearst's International-Cosmopolitan*, September 1931, 148.
48. Putnam, *Soaring Wings*, 160.
49. Earhart, "Why Are Women Afraid to Fly," *Hearst's International-Cosmopolitan*, July 1929, 138.
50. Marguerite Martyn, unknown title, *Post Dispatch* (St. Louis), April 7, 1936, SLRC, microfilm A-129-15.
51. Rich, 229.
52. Earhart, "Flying the Atlantic—and Selling Sausages Have a Lot of Things in Common," *American Magazine*, August 1932, 72.
53. Florence Taaffe, "Miss Earhart, Famed Flier, Arrives in City—by Train," *Minneapolis Tribune*, December 1, 1934. Similar quote: "A Woman in the News," *Christian Science Monitor*, January 16, 1936.
54. Putnam, *Soaring Wings*, 141.
55. "Amelia Earhart, Conqueror of Pacific, Talks Transportation with Akron Women," *Akron (OH) Beacon*, February 14, 1935.
56. Letter from Earhart to Amy Otis Earhart, circa May 1936, SLRC, MC 398, Series I 17.
57. Earhart, *The Fun of It*, 11.

Chapter 11

1. Earhart and Backus, 83.
2. Putnam, *Soaring Wings*, 74.
3. Ibid., 81.
4. Earhart, "My Husband," *Redbook*, September 1932, 23.

5. "Amelia Given Thiel Degree," *McKeesport (PA) Daily News*, December 15, 1932.
6. "Earn Own Living, Miss Earhart Tells Women," *Columbus (OH) Citizen*, January 12, 1934.
7. "Home as Well as Sky Is Amelia's Heaven," unnamed Omaha newspaper, February 19, 1935, Earhart scrapbook 14, GPPC, AESB014.
8. Goerner, 25.
9. Putnam, *Soaring Wings*, 138–39.
10. Butler, 241.
11. "Amelia Earhart Says She Is Not Engaged," *Richmond (VA) Times Dispatch*, November 23, 1928.
12. "Marriage Reports Denied by Aviatrix," *Los Angeles Times*, June 6, 1930.
13. "Amelia Earhart Is to Wed Geo P. Putnam," *Greensboro (NC) Daily News*, November 10, 1930.
14. Letter from Earhart to George Putnam, February 7, 1931, GPPC, b7f150i1.
15. Earhart and Backus, 106.
16. Letter from Earhart to Amy Otis Earhart, February 22, 1931, SLRC, MC 398, Series I 13.
17. "Salons Cheer Amelia, Who Gets Medal," *Seattle Daily Times*, June 21, 1932. Similar quote: "'Amelia Earhart to You' Writers Told 'Not Mrs. Putnam,'" *Omaha World Herald*, June 7, 1935.
18. "Chicago Welcomes Amelia Earhart," *New York Times*, September 23, 1932.
19. Putnam, *Soaring Wings*, 82.
20. "Amelia Earhart Advocates Long Solo Flights as Way to Forget Marital Fights," *Riverside (CA) Daily Press*, March 17, 1936.
21. Putnam, *Soaring Wings*, 87.
22. Rich, 112.
23. Goerner, 25.
24. Earhart, "My Husband," *Redbook*, September 1932, 23.
25. "Should a Wife Support Herself," unknown publication, circa 1930s, GPPC, b9f297i3.
26. "Amelia Earhart Brings Message to Wives; Urges Gainful Work," *Seattle Post-Intelligencer*, February 4, 1933.

27. Putnam, *Soaring Wings*, 144.
28. Goldstein, 84.
29. Letter from Earhart to Amy Otis Earhart, February 1932, SLRC, MC 398, Series I 13.

Chapter 12

1. Earhart, *20 Hrs., 40 Min.*, 32.
2. Ibid., 33.
3. Earhart, "Flying the Atlantic—and Selling Sausages Have a Lot of Things in Common," *American Magazine*, August 1932, 72.
4. Ibid.
5. Earhart, "Why Are Women Afraid to Fly," *Hearst's International-Cosmopolitan*, July 1929, 138.
6. "Miss Earhart in Blackpool," *West Lancashire Evening Gazette* (Blackpool, England), May 23, 1932.
7. Earhart, "Courage," *Survey Graphic*, July 1928, 60.
8. Earhart, "Women and Courage," *Hearst's International-Cosmopolitan*, September 1932, 54.
9. Ibid., 147.
10. Ibid.
11. Ibid., 148. Similar quotes: "Welfare Workers Hail Miss Earhart," *New York Times*, July 9, 1928; "Ride in Traffic Police Car Thrills Miss Earhart," *Boston Daily Globe*, July 8, 1928.
12. Lovell, 190.
13. Earhart, "Flying the Atlantic," *American Magazine*, August 1932, 17.
14. *Green Book*, 1932, SLRC, A-129-15.
15. "City Greets Miss Earhart," *New York Times*, July 7, 1928. Similar quotes: "Miss Earhart's Own Story," *Los Angeles Times*, June 19, 1928; "Girl Flyer Welcomed in New York," *Sunday Tribune* (Providence, RI), July 6, 1928.
16. Earhart, *20 Hrs., 40 Min.*, 47.

17. Earhart, "Fly America First," *Hearst's International-Cosmopolitan*, October 1929, 135.
18. Earhart, "Miss Earhart's Adventure on the Floor of the Sea," *Hearst's International-Cosmopolitan*, November 1929, 102.
19. Earhart, "Women and Courage," *Hearst's International-Cosmopolitan*, September 1932, 148.
20. Daughters of the American Revolution, 655.
21. Putnam, *Soaring Wings*, 171.
22. "'Happy Landing' for Girl Flier," *News Telegram* (Portland, OR), February 1, 1933.
23. Lovell, 215.
24. "Miss Earhart Sets Mark in 2,100-Mile Air Dash from Mexico to Newark," *New York Times*, May 9, 1935. Similar quote: Bertha Arlidge, "Miss Earhart Sees Women Changing," *Journal American* (New York, NY), November 23, 1933.
25. Earhart, "Fly America First," *Hearst's International-Cosmopolitan*, October 1929, 136.
26. Letter from Earhart to Muriel Morrissey, January 31, 1937, SLRC, 83-M69.
27. "Mrs. Putnam Says—," *Graveraet Weekly* (Marquette, MI), October 25, 1932.
28. "Amelia Earhart Putnam Discusses Women in the Field of Aviation," *The Campus* (Sarah Lawrence College, Bronxville, NY), January 23, 1933.
29. "Amelia Earhart Discusses Her Philosophy as a Flyer," *Boston Daily Globe*, February 17, 1935.
30. "Two Ocean Hops Traced," *Los Angeles Times*, March 31, 1935.
31. Earhart, "My Flight from Hawaii," *National Geographic*, May 1935, 607.
32. Richard E. Gnade, "First Lady of Air Relates Adventures during Pacific Hop," *Chautauqua (NY) Daily*, August 10, 1935. Similar quotes: "Flies Because She Enjoys It," unknown newspaper, likely Kansas, circa June 1936, Earhart scrapbook 14, GPPC, AESB014; Louis Schenck, "Amelia Does a Non-Stop," unknown publication, circa 1934–1935, GPPC AESB014.
33. Earhart, *Last Flight*, xvi.

Chapter 13

1. Earhart, *20 Hrs., 40 Min.*, 9.
2. Ibid., 166. Similar quote: Putnam, *Soaring Wings*, 151.
3. Putnam, *Soaring Wings*, 152.
4. Ibid.
5. Ibid., 153.
6. Ibid., 197.
7. Earhart, *The Fun of It*, 55.
8. Ibid., 72.
9. Louis Schenck, "Amelia Does a Non-Stop," unknown publication, circa 1934–1935, Earhart scrapbook 14, GPPC, AESB014.
10. "Amelia Earhart Discusses Her Philosophy as a Flyer," *Boston Daily Globe*, February 17, 1935. Similar quote: "Amelia Earhart Back; Full of Ideas about Young Women," *New York World Telegram*, December 2, 1935.
11. Manthei Howe, "Amelia Earhart Proves Charming Person to Meet and Interview; as Fine Human Being as Aviator," *Daily Mining Journal* (Marquette, MI), October 25, 1932.
12. Earhart, *The Fun of It*, 11.
13. Ware, 101.
14. Earhart, "Let the Best Man Win," *Liberty Magazine*, December 1932, 28.
15. "In Air Race so Her Sex Can Profit," *New York Telegram*, June 30, 1933.
16. Letter from Earhart to Amy Otis Earhart, December 8, 1933, SLRC, MC 398, Series I 15.

Chapter 14

1. Earhart, "Miss Earhart Foresees Planes de Luxe, Due to Women's Interest in Aviation," *New York Times*, June 20, 1928.
2. Earhart, "Miss Earhart Learning What It Is to Be Famous," *Boston Herald*, June 21, 1928.
3. Earhart, "Miss Earhart Predicts Great Airport at Trepassey for Transocean Flights," *New York Times*, June 21, 1928.
4. "Miss Earhart Is Lionized," *New York Times*, June 21, 1928.

5. "Miss Earhart Tires of Being 'Sideshow,'" *New York Times*, July 12, 1928. Similar quote: Earhart, *20 Hrs., 40 Min.*, 115.
6. "Amelia Heads East; Likes Omaha's Field," *Omaha World Herald*, October 12, 1928.
7. Earhart, "Dropping in on England," *McCall's*, October 1928, 21. Similar quote: "Ride in Traffic Police Car Thrills Miss Earhart," *Boston Daily Globe*, July 8, 1928.
8. Earhart, *The Fun of It*, 85.
9. Earhart, *20 Hrs., 40 Min.*, 165.
10. Ibid.
11. Ibid.
12. Putnam, *Soaring Wings*, 165.
13. Letter from Earhart to Ann Morrow Lindbergh, May 8, 1929, GPPC b7f164i1.
14. John M. McCullough, "Miss Earhart Receives 1932 Honor Award," *Philadelphia Inquirer*, October 6, 1932. Similar quote: Lovell, 195.
15. Letter from Earhart to Amy Otis Earhart, January 27, 1933, SLRC, MC 398, Series I 15.
16. "Fame Often Is Tiring Says Amelia Earhart," *Seattle Daily Times*, February 3, 1933.
17. Ibid.
18. Gilroy, 68.
19. Letter from Earhart to Amy Otis Earhart, March 4, 1934, SLRC, MC 398, Series I 16.
20. "Bug Breaks Flight of Miss Earhart," *New York Times*, April 21, 1935.
21. Letter from Earhart to Amy Otis Earhart, circa November 23, 1935, SLRC, MC 398, Series I 16.
22. Janet Mabie, "Amelia Earhart's New Flight," *Christian Science Monitor*, April 29, 1936, 5.
23. *Advocate* (Baton Rouge, LA), May 2, 1936.
24. Letter from Earhart to Amy Otis Earhart, circa March 20 or 23, 1936, SLRC, MC 398, Series I 17.
25. Earhart, *Last Flight*, 59. Similar quote: Earhart, "Flying the Atlantic—and Selling Sausages Have a Lot of Things in Common," *American Magazine*, August 1932, 15.

26. Putnam, *Soaring Wings*, 158.
27. Ibid., 184.
28. Southern, 126.
29. Letter from Earhart to Amy Otis Earhart, August 12, 1928, SLRC, MC 398, Series I 11.
30. Letter from Earhart to Amy Otis Earhart, August 26, 1928, SLRC, MC 398, Series I 11. Similar quote: Letter from Earhart to Amy Otis Earhart, December 26, 1934, SLRC, MC 398, Series I 15.
31. Earhart, *20 Hrs., 40 Min.*, 39.
32. Putnam, *Soaring Wings*, 192.
33. Manthei Howe, "Amelia Earhart Proves Charming Person to Meet and Interview; as Fine Human Being as Aviator," *Daily Mining Journal* (Marquette, MI), October 25, 1932.
34. "Amelia Trusts a Cow and Would Make One Symbol of Aviation," *Boston Daily Globe*, December 14, 1932.
35. "Women Fliers to Help in Next War Miss Earhart Says; North Pole Lures," *Oregonian* (Portland), February 2, 1933.
36. Ibid.
37. Daniel Rochford, "Flying and Flyers," *Boston Transcript*, March 11, 1935.
38. Telegram from Earhart to Eleanor Roosevelt, GPPC b8f237i1, March 14, 1935.
39. Draft of a letter from Earhart to Eleanor Roosevelt, March 14, 1935, GPPC b8f237i4.
40. "Flies Because She Enjoys It," unknown newspaper, likely Kansas, circa June 1936, Earhart scrapbook 14, GPPC AESB014.
41. Letter from Earhart to Amy Otis Earhart, circa May 1936, SLRC, MC 398, Series I 17.
42. "Amelia Earhart Prepares to Fly Round the World," *Christian Science Monitor*, February 12, 1937.

Chapter 15

1. Earhart, "Flying Is Fun," *Hearst's International-Cosmopolitan*, August 1932, 39.

2. Earhart, "Flying the Atlantic—and Selling Sausages Have a Lot of Things in Common," *American Magazine*, August 1932, 17.
3. Ibid.
4. Ibid., 72.
5. Ibid.
6. Putnam, *Soaring Wings*, 47.
7. Ibid., 168.
8. Ibid., 250.
9. Earhart, "Flying the Atlantic—and Selling Sausages Have a Lot of Things in Common," *American Magazine*, August 1932, 72.
10. "Amelia Earhart Resting; Trying to 'Be Herself,'" *Dayton (OH) Daily News*, August 25, 1935.
11. Gordon Sinclair, "'I'm Not a Torch-Bearer' Amelia Earhart Declares," *Toronto Daily Star*, December 12, 1932.
12. Earhart and Backus, 185. Also in Putnam, *Soaring Wings*, 249.
13. Putnam, *Soaring Wings*, 101.
14. Earhart, *Last Flight*, 106.
15. "Hero Worship Not Desired by Aviatrix," *Repository* (Canton, OH), June 20, 1928.
16. Earhart, "Miss Earhart Lonesome for Women in Aviation, She Says," *Boston Herald*, June 22, 1928. Similar quote: Putnam, *Soaring Wings*, 66.
17. Ibid.
18. Letter from Earhart to Amy Otis Earhart, April 20, 1933, SLRC, MC 398, Series I 15.
19. "Amelia Putnam Designs Her Own Sports Clothing," *Omaha (NE) World Herald*, November 24, 1933.
20. Putnam, *Soaring Wings*, 205.
21. Janet Mabie, "Conversations," unnamed publication, Earhart scrapbook 1, GPPC, AESB001.
22. Agnes Fahy, "Flyer Designs Altitude Togs for Air-Minded," *Newark (NJ) Ledger*, January 6, 1934.
23. Janet Mabie, "A Bird's-Eye View of Fashions," *Christian Science Monitor*, February 7, 1934. Similar quotes: "Amelia Earhart, Visitor Here, Discusses Work and Clothes," *Richmond (VA) Times Dispatch*, February 2, 1934; "Unified Control of Transport," *Christian Science Monitor*,

March 16, 1934; Gertrude Bailey, "Amelia Earhart, Our Newest Designer Presents Air-Minded Creations," *New York World Telegram*, December 23, 1933.
24. Ibid.
25. "Amelia Earhart Busy Breaking Precedents; Now She Tries a Hand at Dress Designing," *Springfield (MA) Republican*, May 18, 1934. Also in Sigrid Arne, "She Breaks Precedent," *Richmond (VA) Times Dispatch*, May 15, 1934.
26. "Famous Flyer Tells of Hop over Pacific," unknown Marion newspaper, likely Illinois, February 22, 1935, Earhart scrapbook 14, GPPC, AESB014.
27. Earhart, *20 Hrs., 40 Min.*, 2–5.
28. Earhart, *The Fun of It*, 18.
29. Earhart, "Women and Courage," *Hearst's International-Cosmopolitan*, September 1932, 55.
30. "Flying Doesn't Thrill Amelia—It's Scenery," *Milwaukee (WI) Journal*, October 29, 1932.
31. Earhart, *The Fun of It*, 138.
32. "There's Just This One Flight Left in My System," *Boston Daily Globe*, September 26, 1937.
33. Earhart, *Last Flight*, xvi.
34. Thaden, Louise, 150.
35. "Noted Woman Pilot to Talk on 'Sky Adventures,'" *Jewish Chronicle* (Newark, NJ), January 3, 1936.
36. Earhart, *The Fun of It*, 27.
37. Letter from Earhart to Amy Otis Earhart, circa May 6, 1936, SLRC, MC 398, Series I 17. The European trip is disclosed in a May 9, 1936, letter from Earhart to Amy Otis Earhart, SLRC, MC 398, Series I 17.
38. Earhart, *The Fun of It*, 83.
39. Earhart, "Fly Fishing," *Outdoor Life*, December 1934, 62.
40. Earhart, *Last Flight*, 39.
41. Lovell, 179.
42. Earhart, *20 Hrs., 40 Min.*, 168.
43. Mortimer Franklin, "Amelia Earhart Looks at the Films!" *Screenland*, June 1933, 29.

44. Ibid., 30.
45. Earhart, "Part of the Fun of It," *Vanity Fair*, April 1933, 19.
46. Ibid, 19.
47. Earhart, *Last Flight*, 80.
48. Ibid., 81.
49. "Women Trained as Pilots Compare Favorably with Men, Belief Expressed by Amelia Earhart Putnam," *Enid (OK) Morning Times*, circa 1931, Earhart scrapbook 3, GPPC, AESB003.
50. "Miss Earhart Says 'Flying Clothes' Are Unnecessary for Women," *New York Times*, June 22, 1928.
51. Earhart, *Last Flight*, 82.
52. Amelia Earhart to Kenneth Griggs Merrill, 1918–1919, SLRC, A/M571.
53. "Miss Earhart Wins Acclaim in Non-stop Mexican Flight," *Trenton (NJ) Evening Times*, May 9, 1935.
54. Earhart, *20 Hrs., 40 Min.*, 79.
55. Letter from Earhart to Amy Otis Earhart, December 8, 1933, SLRC, MC 398, Series I 15.
56. "To Air," *Toledo (OH) News-Bee*, July 23, 1928.
57. Backus, 51.
58. Southern, 105.
59. Putnam, *Soaring Wings*, 48
60. Earhart, *20 Hrs., 40 Min.*, 81.
61. Lovell, 107.
62. Letter from Earhart to Amy Otis Earhart, May 20, 1928, GPPC, b7f145i3.
63. Letter from Earhart to Edwin S. Earhart, May 20, 1928, GPPC, b7f146i1.
64. "Miss Earhart Made Her Will Before Start," *New York Times*, June 5, 1928.

Chapter 16

1. Letter from Earhart to Amy Otis Earhart, October 15, 1916, SLRC, MC 398, Series I 7.

2. Letter from Earhart to Amy Otis Earhart, November 1917, SLRC, MC 398, Series I 9.
3. Earhart, "Miss Earhart Foresees Planes de Luxe, Due to Women's Interest in Aviation," *New York Times*, June 20, 1928.
4. Earhart, *20 Hrs., 40 Min.*, 106.
5. "New York Hails Amelia Earhart as 'Lady Lindy,'" *Christian Science Monitor*, July 6, 1928.
6. "Amelia a 'Social Worker on a Bat," *Plain Dealer* (Cleveland, OH), July 8, 1928.
7. "Miss Earhart Shies at Air Meet's Peril," *New York Times*, September 15, 1928.
8. Earhart, "Dropping in on England," *McCall's*, October 1928, 21. Similar quote: "Miss Earhart and Partner Take Private Car to New York," *Boston Herald*, July 11, 1928.
9. Earhart, *20 Hrs., 40 Min.*, 4. Also in Grace Farrington Gray, "We're Off," *The Farmer's Wife*, August 1935, 6.
10. Ferris, 5.
11. Ibid.
12. Ibid., 6.
13. Ibid., 5.
14. Laura Benham, "Amelia Earhart Answers the Call of Fate," *Illustrated Love Magazine*, January 1932, 24.
15. Earhart, "Flying the Atlantic—and Selling Sausages Have a Lot of Things in Common," *American Magazine*, August 1932, 72.
16. "Scenes of Mrs. Amelia Earhart Putnam's Visit Here to Lecture before Business and Professional Women," *Springfield (MA) Daily Republican*, December 9, 1932.
17. Gordon Sinclair, "'I'm Not a Torch-Bearer' Amelia Earhart Declares," *Toronto Daily Star*, December 12, 1932.
18. Ibid.
19. Dawson, 41.
20. Putnam, *Soaring Wings*, 165–66.
21. Ibid., 166.
22. "Fame Often Is Tiring Says Amelia Earhart," *Seattle Daily Times*, February 3, 1933.

23. Earhart, "Fly Fishing," *Outdoor Life*, December 1934, 16.
24. "Amelia Earhart Is Helping Youth," unknown publication, circa 1934–1935, Earhart scrapbook 3, GPPC, AESB003.
25. Putnam, *Soaring Wings*, 258.
26. Arthur Brisbane, "Today—Views of News," *San Diego Union*, January 14, 1935.
27. "Amelia Earhart, Conqueror of Pacific, Talks Transportation with Akron Women," *Akron (OH) Beacon*, February 14, 1935.
28. "Famous Flyer Tells of Hop over Pacific," unknown Marion, Indiana, newspaper, February 22, 1935, Earhart scrapbook 14, GPPC AESB014.
29. "Amelia Plans to Equal All Aviation Records Achieved by Male Pilots," *Boston Daily Globe*, May 24, 1935. Similar quote: "Miss Earhart's Goal," *Boston Herald*, May 24, 1935.
30. Richard E. Gnade, "First Lady of Air Relates Adventures during Pacific Hop," *Chautauqua (NY) Daily*, August 10, 1935.
31. "Amelia Earhart Resting; Trying to 'Be Herself,'" *Dayton (OH) Daily News*, August 25, 1935.
32. Grace Farrington Gray, "We're Off," *The Farmer's Wife*, 6.
33. "Footnote on Fame," *State Times Advocate* (Baton Rouge, LA), March 5, 1936. Similar quotes: Earhart, *The Fun of It*, 100; Putnam, *Soaring Wings*, 93.
34. Lovell, 234.
35. "Amelia Earhart Back in City," *Los Angeles Times*, March 26, 1937.
36. "Lack of Beauty Turned Miss Earhart to Flying," *Omaha (NE) World Herald*, July 13, 1937.
37. Putnam, *Soaring Wings*, 294.
38. Undated clipping, "Amelia Earhart Declares Aviators Are Not Thrill Seekers," *Huntington (IN) Herald Press*, GPPC, XV.G.4.
39. "Amelia Earhart Here in New Role of Fashion Designer for Women," *Boston Daily Globe*, January 25, 1934.
40. "Amelia Earhart Discusses Her Philosophy as a Flyer," *Boston Daily Globe*, February 17, 1935.
41. "Lack of Beauty Turned Miss Earhart to Flying," *Omaha World Herald*, July 13, 1937.
42. Earhart, *Last Flight*, 46.

Chapter 17

1. Putnam, *Soaring Wings*, 122.
2. Earhart, *20 Hrs., 40 Min.*, 23.
3. Undated note from Earhart to Amy Otis Earhart, SLRC, MC 398, Series I 18.
4. Letter from Earhart to Amy Otis Earhart, October 2, 1930, SLRC, MC 398, Series I 12.
5. Earhart, *The Fun of It*, 170.
6. Putnam, *Soaring Wings*, 185.
7. "Amelia Earhart, Visitor Here, Discusses Work and Clothes," *Richmond (VA) Times Dispatch*, February 2, 1934.
8. Putnam, *Soaring Wings*, 184.
9. Letter from Earhart to Amy Otis Earhart, circa March 20 or 23, 1936, SLRC, MC 398, Series I 17.
10. "Loafing along in a Giro," *World-Herald* (Omaha, NE), June 1, 1931.
11. "Amelia Planning No Globe Flight; She Is Wondering about Her Luck," *Omaha World Herald*, February 19, 1935.
12. "Amelia Earhart Would Have Flown Anywhere with Post at Controls," *Boston Daily Globe*, August 19, 1935.
13. Earhart, "Wiley Post," *Forum*, October 1935, 196.
14. Chapman, 6.
15. Earhart, "My Lucky Turning Point," *Boston Herald*, April 28, 1935.
16. Laura Benham, "Amelia Earhart Answers the Call of Fate," *Illustrated Love Magazine*, January 1932, 113.
17. "Harrison, Rye Give Royal Welcome to Amelia Earhart Putnam," *Daily Item* (Chester, NY), June 28, 1932.
18. Lovell, 197.
19. Earhart, *Last Flight*, 41.
20. Putnam, *Wide Margins*, 283.
21. Daughters of the American Revolution, 661. Similar quote: "Mrs. Putnam Gibes at D.A.R. on Arms," *New York Times*, April 22, 1933.
22. Ware, 119.

Chapter 18

1. "A Useless Adventure," *Aeroplane*, January 16, 1935, 61.
2. Earhart, *Last Flight*, 50.
3. "Lady Astor Lauds Amelia Earhart," *New York Times*, June 28, 1928.
4. Tate, 137.
5. "Their Champion," *Boston Daily Globe*, June 20, 1932.
6. Arthur Brisbane, "Today Views of News," *San Diego Union*, May 22, 1932.
7. "Dropping in on England," *McCall's*, October 1928, 21.
8. "Hoover Leads Nation in Praise of Flight," *Boston Daily Globe*, May 22, 1932.
9. Amelia Earhart's FBI file, 30, http://vault.fbi.gov/amelia-mary-earhart/amelia-mary-earhart-part-01-of-01/view.
10. Telegram from Carrie Chapman Catt to Earhart, June 19, 1932, III.C.13, GPPC.
11. Lovell, 240.
12. Planck, 220.
13. Letter to Earhart from Calvin Coolidge, June 18, 1932, I.D.5, GPPC.
14. George Palmer Putnam, "The Forgotten Husband," *Pictorial Review*, December 1932.
15. Earhart, "Miss Earhart Learning What It Is to Be Famous," *Boston Herald*, June 21, 1928. Similar quote: "I thought she had too much sense to try it," Rich, 69.
16. "Mrs. Earhart Calm on Hearing of Feat," *New York Times*, July 19, 1928.
17. Winters, 105.
18. Southern, 112.
19. "Miss Earhart's Dad Talks," *Los Angeles Times*, June 18, 1928.
20. Ibid.
21. "Father Says Miss Earhart Learned to Fly without His Knowledge," *Tampa (FL) Tribune*, June 19, 1928.
22. "Dad Proud of Air Heroine," *Los Angeles Times*, June 19, 1928.
23. Furman, 95.

24. Butler, 273.
25. "London Crowds Rush to Greet Atlantic Fliers," *Christian Science Monitor*, June 20, 1928.
26. "Tributes Are Paid to Amelia Earhart," *New York Times*, November 22, 1937.
27. Telegram to Earhart from Herbert Hoover, May 21, 1932, III.C.30.B, GPPC.
28. Putnam, *Soaring Wings*, 126–27.
29. Ibid., 127.
30. Jenkinson, 262.
31. Sinclair Lewis, "This Golden Half Century," *Good Housekeeping*, May 1935, 262.
32. Lindbergh, *Hour of Gold, Hour of Lead*, 121.
33. Lindbergh, *Locked Rooms and Open Doors*, 5.
34. Berg, 278.
35. Lovell, 255.
36. "Miss Earhart's Name Figures in Divorce," *Trenton Evening Times*, March 3, 1936.
37. National American Suffrage Association, 132.
38. Ware, 54.
39. "Amelia Earhart," *New York Times*, July 20, 1937.
40. "About All She Has Proved," *New York Post*, May 21, 1932.
41. "Harrison, Rye Give Royal Welcome to Amelia Earhart Putnam," *Daily Item* (Chester, NY), June 28, 1932.
42. "Receives Pictures Sent from Java," *Springfield (MA) Republican*, July 8, 1937.
43. Ware, 86.
44. Ibid.
45. "Feminists Stirred over Women Flier," *New York Times*, November 8, 1935.
46. "Promised Director Return to Her Work," *New York Times*, June 19, 1928.
47. Rich, 119.
48. "Calls Miss Earhart Modest and Charming," *New York Times*, June 18, 1928.
49. Chapman, 120.

50. Ibid., 129.
51. Ibid., 167.
52. Ibid., 180.
53. "Amelia Earhart Weds," *Omaha World Herald*, February 8, 1931.
54. Chapman, 188.
55. "Mother-in-Law of Amelia Pays Visit," *Press-Scimitar* (Memphis, TN), September 22, 1932.
56. Lovell, 98.
57. Putnam, *Andrée, the Record of a Tragic Adventure*, dedication page.
58. "Putnam Marries Amelia Earhart," *Boston Daily Globe*, February 8, 1931.
59. "Marriage Will Not Check Her Career in Air, Amelia Earhart Informs the Public," *Greensboro (NC) Record*, February 18, 1931.
60. "Lesser Halves of Famous Wives," *New York World Telegram*, February 8, 1932.
61. Rich, 151.
62. "Miss Earhart in London," *Sunday Mail*, May 22, 1932.
63. "Amelia Earhart Lands Plane in Irish Farmyard," *Tampa (FL) Sunday Tribune*, May 22, 1932.
64. George Palmer Putnam, "The Forgotten Husband," *Pictorial Review*, December 1932.
65. George Palmer Putnam, "A Flyer's Husband," *Forum*, June 1935, 330. Similar quote: "Putnam Married Life Fraught with Suspense," *Springfield (MA) Republican*, July 8, 1937.
66. Lovell, 243.
67. Letter to Earhart from George Putnam, circa 1937, b7f155i1, GPPC.
68. Letter to Earhart from George Putnam, circa 1937, b7f155i2, GPPC.
69. Putnam, *Soaring Wings*, 24.
70. Putnam, *Wide Margins*, 282.
71. Ibid., 283.
72. "Will Thinks Huey Has Big Chance to Prove Something," *Plain Dealer* (Cleveland, OH), April 19, 1935.
73. Will Rogers, *Montana Standard* (Butte), August 4, 1935.
74. Will Rogers, "Will Durant Is a 'Regular Guy' Says Will Rogers," *Omaha World Herald*, August 4, 1935.

75. Butler, 281.
76. Gilroy, 53. Similar quote: Amelia Earhart's FBI file, 25, http://vault.fbi.gov/amelia-mary-earhart/amelia-mary-earhart-part-01-of-01/view.
77. Letter from Franklin Delano Roosevelt to Earhart, January 18, 1935, GPPC, b438i.
78. "Roosevelt Sends Felicitations to Amelia Earhart," *Dallas Morning News*, January 20, 1935.
79. Lovell, 140.
80. *The American Experience: Amelia Earhart* (Boston, MA: PBS video, WGBH/Boston, Nancy Porter Productions, 1993).
81. Smith, 73–74.
82. "Daring Aviatrix a Real Old Fashioned Girl," *Pittsburgh Press*, June 5, 1928.
83. Thaden, 147.
84. Ibid., 150.
85. Untitled article, *Richmond (VA) Times Dispatch*, July 9, 1937.
86. "Feminists Dislike Earhart Welcome," unknown publication, Earhart Scrapbook 3, AESB003, GPPC. For more about Lady Margaret Heath (editor of *Tide and Time*), see Lindie Naughton, *Lady Icarus: The Life of Irish Aviator Lady Mary Heath*.
87. Rich, 139.
88. Ibid., 106.
89. *The American Experience: Amelia Earhart* (Boston, MA: PBS video, WGBH/Boston, Nancy Porter Productions, 1993).
90. "Welfare Workers Hail Miss Earhart," *New York Times*, July 9, 1928.
91. "Flyer Began Her Exploring as Little Girl," *San Francisco Chronicle*, September 20, 1937.
92. "Al Williams Rips Earhart 'Stunt' Flying," *Cleveland Press*, March 31, 1937. Response: *New York Herald Tribune*, April 7, 1937. See also Putnam, *Soaring Wings*, 198–99.

Bibliography

Archives

SLRC   Amelia Earhart Papers, Schlesinger Library, Radcliffe Institute, Harvard University, Cambridge, MA

GPPC George Putnam Collection of Amelia Earhart Papers, Archives and Special Collections, Purdue University Library, West Lafayette, IN

FDRL   Franklin D. Roosevelt Presidential Library and Museum, Hyde Park, NY

Primary and Secondary Sources

Alexander, Anna, and Mark S. Roberts. *High Culture: Reflections on Addiction and Modernity*. Albany: State University of New York Press, 2003.

Becker, Susan D. *The Origins of the Equal Rights Amendment: American Feminism between the Wars*. Westport, CT: Greenwood Press, 1981.

Bell, Elizabeth S. *Sisters of the Wind: Voices of Early Women Aviators*. Pasadena, CA: Trilogy Books, 1994.

Berg, A. Scott. *Lindbergh*. New York: G. P. Putman's Sons, 1998.

Brady, Tim. *The American Aviation Experience: A History*. Carbondale: Southern Illinois University Press, 2000.

Briand, Paul Jr. *Daughter of the Sky: The Story of Amelia Earhart*. New York: Duell, Sloane and Pearce, 1960.

Burke, John. *Winged Legend: The Story of Amelia Earhart*. New York: G. P. Putnam's Sons, 1970.

Butler, Susan. *East to the Dawn: The Life of Amelia Earhart*. Reading, MA: Addison-Wesley, 1997.

Chapman, Sally Putnam, and Stephanie Mansfield. *Whistled Like a Bird: The Untold Story of Dorothy Putnam, George Putnam, and Amelia Earhart*. New York: Warner Books, 1997.

Corn, Joseph J. *The Winged Gospel: America's Romance with Aviation, 1900–1950*. New York: Oxford University Press, 1982.

Courtwright, David T. *Sky as Frontier: Adventure, Aviation, and Empire*. College Station: Texas A&M University Press, 2005.

Crouch, Tom D. *Wing: A History of Aviation from Kites to the Space Age*. New York: W. W. Norton & Company, 2004.

Daughters of the American Revolution. *Proceedings of the Forty-second Continental Congress of the National Society of the D.A.R.* Washington, DC: Press of Judd & Detweiler, 1933.

Dawson, Virginia P., and Mark D. Bowles, eds. *Realizing the Dream of Flight*. Washington, DC: National Aeronautics and Space Administration, 2005.

Dumenil, Lynn. *The Modern Temper: American Culture and Society in the 1920s*. New York: Hill and Wang, 1995.

Dwiggins, Don. *Hollywood Pilot: The Biography of Paul Mantz*. New York: Doubleday & Company, 1967.

Earhart, Amelia. *20 Hrs., 40 Min.: Our Flight in the Friendship*. 1928. Reprint, Washington, DC: National Geographic Society, 2003.

———. *The Fun of It*. 1932. Reprint, Chicago, IL: Academy Press Limited, 1977.

———. *Last Flight*. 1937. Reprint, New York: Crown Trade Paperbacks, 1988.

Earhart, Amelia, and Jean L. Backus. *Letters from Amelia: An Intimate Portrait of Amelia Earhart*. Boston, MA: Beacon Press, 1982.

Faulkner, Carol. *Lucretia Mott's Heresy: Abolition and Women's Rights in Nineteenth-Century America*. Philadelphia: University of Pennsylvania Press, 2001.

Ferris, Helen. *Five Girls Who Dared*. 1931. Reprint, New York: Books for Libraries Press, 1971.

Furman, Bess. *Washington By-Line: The Personal History of a Newspaperwoman*. New York: Harcourt Brace Jovanovich, 1977.

Gillespie, Ric. *Finding Amelia: The True Story of the Earhart Disappearance*. Annapolis, MD: Naval Institute Press, 2006.

Gilroy, Shirley Dobson. *Amelia: Pilot in Pearls*. MacLean, VA: Link Press, 1985.

Goerner, Fred. *The Search for Amelia Earhart*. Garden City, NJ: Doubleday & Company, 1966.

Goldstein, Donald M., and Katherine V. Dillon. *Amelia: The Centennial Biography of an Aviation Pioneer*. Washington, DC: Brassey's, 1997.

Harrison, James P. *Mastering the Sky: A History of Aviation from Ancient Times to the Present*. New York: De Capo Press, 2000.

Jenkinson, Anthony. *America Came My Way*. London: A Barker, 1936.

Johnson, E. R. *American Flying Boats and Amphibious Aircraft: An Illustrated History*. Jefferson, NC: McFarland & Company, 2009.

Koziara, Karen Shallcross, Michael H. Moskow, and Lucretia Dewey Tanner. *Working Women: Past, Present, Future*. Washington, DC: Bureau of National Affairs, 1987.

Lawrence, Harry. *Aviation and the Role of Government*. Dubuque, IA: Kendall Hunt, 2004.

Lindbergh, Anne Morrow. *Hour of Gold, Hour of Lead: Diaries and Letters of Anne Morrow Lindbergh, 1929–1932*. New York: Harcourt Brace Jovanovich, 1973.

———. *Locked Rooms and Open Doors*. New York: Harcourt, Brace & Jovanovich, 1993.

Long, Elgen M., and Marie K. Long. *Amelia Earhart: The Mystery Solved*. New York: Simon & Schuster, 1999.

Lovell, Mary S. *The Sound of Wings: The Life of Amelia Earhart*. New York: St. Martin's Press, 1989.

Lubben, Kristen, Erin Barnett, and Susan Butler. *Amelia Earhart: Image and Icon*. New York: International Center of Photography, 2007.

Morrissey, Muriel Earhart, and Carol L. Osborne. *Amelia, My Courageous Sister*. Santa Clara, CA: Osborne Publisher, 1987.

National American Woman Suffrage Association Collection. *Changing Standards: Report of the Fourth Annual New York Herald Tribune Women's Conference on Current Problems*. New York: New York Herald Tribune, 1934.

National Society of the Daughters of the American Revolution. *Proceedings of the Forty-Second Continental Congress*. Washington, DC: Daughters of the American Revolution, 1933.

Naughton, Lindie. *Lady Icarus: The Life of Irish Aviator Lady Mary Heath*. Dublin: Ashfield Press, 2004.

Nichols, Ruth. *Wings for Life*. Philadelphia, PA: J. B. Lippincott Company, 1957.

Planck, Charles E. *Women with Wings*. New York: Harper & Brothers, 1942.

Putnam, George Palmer. *Andree: The Record of a Tragic Adventure*. New York: Brewer & Warren, 1930.

———. *Soaring Wings: A Biography of Amelia Earhart*. New York: Harcourt, Brace and Company, 1939.

———. *Wide Margins: A Publisher's Autobiography*. New York: Harcourt, Brace and Company, 1942.

Rich, Doris L. *Amelia Earhart: A Biography*. Washington, DC: Smithsonian Institution, 1989.

Russell, Dora. *The Right to Be Happy*. New York: Harper & Brothers, 1927.

Sherman, Janann. *Walking on Air: The Aerial Adventures of Phoebe Omlie*. Jackson: University of Mississippi Press, 2011.

Smith, Elinor. *Aviatrix*. New York: Harcourt Brace Jovanovich, 1981.

Southern, Neta Snook. *I Taught Amelia to Fly*. New York: Vantage Press, 1974.

Tate, Grover Ted. *The Lady Who Tamed Pegasus: The Story of Pancho Barnes*. New York: Aviation Book Company, 1984.

Thaden, Louise. *High, Wide, and Frightened*. Fayetteville: University of Arkansas Press, 2004.

Van Pelt, Lori. *Amelia Earhart: The Sky Is No Limit*. New York: Forge, 2005.

Van Riper, A. Bowdoin. *Imagining Flight: Aviation and Popular Culture*. College Station: Texas A&M University Press, 2004.

Ware, Susan. *Still Missing: Amelia Earhart and the Search for Modern Feminism*. New York: W. W. Norton & Company, 1993.

Winters, Kathleen C. *Amelia Earhart: The Turbulent Life of an American Icon*. New York: Palgrave MacMillan, 2010.

Index

ability, 17, 104
accidents, 37–38, 48, 157
actress, 142
advancement, 105
adventure, 22, 24, 26, 36, 108, 151–53, 187, 188, 189
Aeroplane, 184
Africa, 161
age, 34, 36, 84, 173
airmail, 41
airplanes, 6–8, 13, 17, 46–48, 55, 84, 157, 169
airports, 46, 48, 54
airway, 42
Albert I, 175
alcohol, 101, 133, 134, 176
Allen, C. B., 184
ambition, 124
anxiety, 130
applesauce, 32, 145
appliances, 104
aptitude, 104
aristocrat, 176
armaments, 83, 84
arms lobbyists, 84
army. *See* military
artifacts, 158
Astor, Nancy, 142, 184
Atchison, Kansas, xiii
atheist, 163
Atlantic, 151, 152
autogiro, xiv, 2, 9, 37, 46
autographs, 141, 142
automobile, 4, 5, 10, 12, 13, 53–55, 127, 128, 141, 172
aviation, 5, 12, 13, 24, 42–45, 109, 114, 154, 155, 160, 167, 171, 172, 173, 193. *See also* flying
aviation industry, 12, 13, 15, 41–48, 84, 85, 94, 108, 171, 172

aviator. *See* pilot
aviatrix. *See* pilot
Avro Avian, xiv
ax, 16

baggage, 23, 27
Bailey, Mary, 202
Barnes, Florence "Pancho," 184
barnstorming, 1
bathing suit, 194
beauty, 4, 11, 44, 153, 201
beauty shops, 153
Bendix Trophy, 29
birth control, 112, 113, 119–20
Boll, Mabel, 19, 22
books, 92–94
bootlegger, 24
Boston, xiii
Boston and Maine Railroad, 42
Boston Daily Globe, xi, 139, 185
boxer shorts, 112
bred to timidity, 102, 112
broomstick, 117
Bryn Mawr, 90
bug, 32
bundle, 20, 202
bunk, 140
Bureau of Aeronautics, 36
Bureau of Air Commerce, 14, 37, 75, 172, 202
business, 14, 57–58, 114, 117, 170
Butterball, 167
Byrd, Richard, 133, 146, 185

cage, 113, 116
California, 29
camels, 154
car. *See* automobile
Caraway, Hattie W., 186
Catt, Carrie Chapman, 186
challenge, 103
Chapman, Sam, 111, 115, 146
children. *See* youth
chivalry, 86, 106
cigarettes, 133, 134, 146
circus, 6, 42
civilization, 82
civilized barbarism, 82
Clark, Earnest C., 30
clothes, 154–56, 194, 203
Cochran, Jacqueline, 186
coffee, 135
Coleman, Bessie, x
colors, 156, 191
Columbia University, xiii, 51, 89
combat, 83
common sense, 152
competition, 6
confidence, 124
cooking, 68, 90
Coolidge, Calvin, 182, 186, 202
Cooper, Phil, 187
Cornell, Katherine, 172
courage, 23, 125–26, 185, 190
coward, 125
cowardice, 31
cows, 28, 147

crashes, 17, 33, 141
criticism, 30, 31, 103, 141, 173
Crosson Marvel, 25, 157
Crusades, 85
curiosities, 16
cyclone cellar, 115

Dakar, 161
dancing, 10, 82, 156
danger, 172
Daughters of the American Revolution, 81, 83, 180
death, 157
Denison House, xiii, 58, 194
Depression (Great Depression), 59, 77, 156
desires, 126
dieting, 173
disappearance, ix, x
discovery, 52
discrimination, 105–6, 107
divorce, 118, 178
draft, 81, 83, 86
dreams, 3, 11, 127
drowning, 157
dysentery, 35

Earhart, Amelia: as author, 92–93; childhood, 57, 169; education, 89, 167, 170; flights of, xiii–xv, 19–39; Hawaii to California flight, xv, 21, 29, 30, 31, 38, 148, 171, 184; jobs, 65; round-the-world flight, ix, 184, 201; transatlantic crossing (1928), 22–25, 175, 188; transatlantic crossing (1932), 25–28, 160, 179, 185, 190, 192, 196, 197, 198, 202
Earhart, Amy Otis, 32, 34, 57, 58, 61–62, 65, 93, 111, 117, 119, 120, 143, 144, 158, 164–65, 175–76, 177, 187
Earhart, Edwin, 57, 111, 146, 164, 176, 187
Earhart, Muriel. *See* Morrissey, Muriel Earhart
economics, 59–61, 104, 107
ego, 33
Elder, Ruth, 20
elders, 108, 109
Electra airplane. *See* Lockheed Electra
engineering, 89
engines, 52, 55
England, 148, 161
Enid (Oklahoma), 161
equality, 108, 112
equal rights, 107, 115
evolution, 77
exercise, 133, 135
experience, 11, 92
experimenting, 108
exploration, 158

failure, 36
fame, 139–48, 202

family, 158
family bus, 7
fear, 127–28
feminist, 13, 97, 107, 197
film, 84, 170
fisherman, 170
fling, 35
flivver, 7
flying, 1–17, 43, 59, 60, 107, 155, 157, 169, 171, 173, 176, 179, 180. *See also* aviation
flying age, 3
Flying Laboratory, 204
fog, 31
food, 133, 134, 135, 147–48, 162, 173
France, 148, 162
freedom, 4, 76, 98, 103, 156
free love, 112
Friendship, xiv, 19, 27, 111, 146, 158, 168, 188
frontiers, 153
fun, 34, 58, 68, 118
The Fun of It, xi, xiv
Furman, Bess, 188
future, 34, 46–48, 54–55, 82

gambling, 28
garages, 48
Garbo, Greta, 203
gasoline, 27
gender, 98–101, 105, 106
Germany, 162
Gilbreth, Lillian Moller, 188
glory, 17
goldfish, 142
Gordon, Louis, xiv, 19, 25
government, 45, 75–78, 180
Grayson, Frances, 20
Guest, Amy Phipps, 19, 24, 188

Hamlet, 130
Hawaii, xv, 21, 29, 30, 31, 38, 148, 171, 190
Hearst, Fanny, 189
Heath, Mary, xiv, 202
heredity, 16
hero, 125, 171
heroine, 94
history, 158
home, 104
homestead, 146
Hoover, Herbert, 26, 74, 189
Hoover, Lou Henry, 190
hope, 124
horse and buggy, 128
horseback riding, 172
housework, 71–73, 100–101
Howland Island, xv, 21, 33, 34, 76
hunting, 159
hussies, 69
Hyde Park High School, xiii

icebox, 147
ideas, 108
ignorance, 102
illness, 136

imagination, 5, 45
impossible, 102
inbred timidity, 102, 111, 170
incompetence, 6
individualism, 54, 104
Industrial Revolution, 65
Industrial Workers of the World, 78
industry, 69, 78, 104, 180
inferiority, 12
inquisitiveness, 105
instruments, 8, 11, 28
intelligence, 123
invention, 71
Ireland, 20, 26, 27
Islam, 163
Itasca, 35

Japanese, ix
Jenkinson, Anthony, 190
Johnson, x
junket, 83

killing, 159
Kinnear Airster biplane, xiii
Kissel, 51
Kitty Hawk, 1

Lady Lindy, x, 143, 168
Last Flight, xi
legislation, 71, 77, 78, 104, 107, 108
Lewis, Sinclair, 190
Liberty Bonds, 82

life, 22, 159
Lindbergh, Ann Morrow, x, 16, 143, 176, 191
Lindbergh, Charles, x, xiv, 1, 16, 20, 59, 143, 168, 172, 176, 177, 188, 191, 192, 201, 203
Lockheed Electra 10E, 8, 36, 38, 40, 96
Lockheed Vega 5B, xiv
Los Angeles, 21, 28
lost generation, 192
love, 128, 179, 198
luck, 128–29
Lucky Strikes, 133, 134, 146
Lucy Stone League, 112. *See also* Stone, Lucy
Ludington Line. *See* New York-Philadelphia-Washington Airways

machine age, 52, 104
machines, 4, 5, 51–55, 65, 90, 180
mail, 142, 143
male supremacy, 107
Manning, Harry, 191
Mantz, Myrtle, 145, 177, 192
Mantz, Paul, 101, 177, 192
marriage, 15, 16, 60, 68, 70, 72, 73, 98, 105, 113–18, 141, 142, 195, 196
martyrdom, 179
mascot, 159
material age, 109
McCallion, Dan, 26

McCall's, 24, 142, 146, 168, 185
mechanics, 68, 99, 159
Meelie, 167, 187
Meloney, Marie Mattingly, 192
men, 14, 15, 17, 23, 36, 52, 69, 98–101, 103, 104, 105, 113, 115, 185, 190, 193; as fathers, 98, 100–101, 113, 118–19, 197
Mexico, xv, 21, 32, 144, 162
Miami, Florida, xv
military, 14, 15, 17
misanthrope, 142
money, 4, 6, 57–62, 90, 153
morale, 126
Morrissey, Muriel Earhart ("Pidge"), 2, 58, 61–62, 65, 93, 117, 119, 120, 144, 192
mother's milk, 103
motorcar. *See* automobile
motorcycle police officers, 159
Mott, Lucretia, 106
movies, 160, 170
musketeers, 25

National Aeronautic Association, xiv, 25
National Air Races, xv, 29
National Geographic Society, xiv
National Woman's Party, 97, 105–6, 108
nerves, 102
Newark, 21, 28, 32, 162
New Deal, 75

Newfoundland, 19, 162
Newman, Paul, 203
new social order, 77, 109
New York-Philadelphia-Washington Airways (Ludington Line), xiv, 42
New York Post, 192
New York Times, 193
Nichols, Ruth, x, 20, 29, 38, 177, 193
Ninety-Nines, xiv
Noonan, Fred, ix, 33, 34, 193
novices, 151
Noyes, Blanche, x, 193
nurse, 80

oatmeal, 135
Old Bessie, 29
Olympics, 136
Omlie, Phoebe, 194
opportunity, 105
optimism, 129
ox cart, 128

pacifism, 81
parachutes, 2, 9, 35
parasites, 69
parenting, 98, 102, 104, 113, 118–19, 126
parsley on a lamb chop, 169
Paul, Alice Stokes, 194
peace, 109
pensions, 78
peppers, 140

Perkins, Marion, 194
photography, 160
pigeonholes, 91
pilot, 5, 10–17, 21, 29, 106, 128, 130, 135, 142, 170, 175, 199
pioneer, 12, 154, 158
poetry, 8, 125, 128, 172
politics, 54, 75–78, 97
"popping off" letters, 164–65
Post, Wiley, 32, 177–78
poverty, 59, 62
power, 129
prejudice, 12, 14, 15
prenuptial letter, 112, 116
president, 98
press, x, 34, 97, 123, 139, 145–48, 183
prima donna, 191
Prohibition, 24, 134
propaganda, 83
protection, 105
psychiatrists, 92
psychologists, 92
puppets, 145
Purdue University, 50, 65, 88, 91, 96, 150
Purdue University Airport, 56, 110
Putnam, David Binney, 194
Putnam, Dorothy (Dorothy Binney Putnam Upton Blanding Palmer), 178, 195–96
Putnam, Frances Faulkner, 196
Putnam, George Palmer, xiv, 20, 25, 34, 35, 37, 57, 110, 112, 115–18, 144, 146, 173, 178–79, 183, 184, 186, 195, 196–99, 200

rabbits' feet, 129
radio, 2, 47, 109, 168
railroad, 53, 171
Rasche, Thea, 19
reading, 93–94, 173
records, 38–39, 107, 169
religion, 163
reporters, x, 97, 123, 139, 145–48, 183
retirement, 73
Right to Be Happy, 102, 111, 170
risks, 34, 126
Rogers, Will, 178, 199
roller coaster, 9, 51
romance, 3, 4, 43, 44, 85
Roosevelt, Eleanor, xi, 75, 77, 144, 147–48, 172, 173, 174, 180, 199–200, 203
Roosevelt, Franklin Delano, 75, 76, 77, 78, 180, 200
Rosie the Riveter, x
ruffles, 156
Russell, Dora, 102, 111, 170

sabotage, 30
sack of potatoes, 27
safety, 8, 9
salt, 113
sandwiches, 135
Sanger, Margaret, 113
scatterbrains, 151
science, 71, 72, 77, 100, 171

secret, 158
security, 103
Senate Air Safety Committee, 144
sewing, 102, 155, 173
sex. *See* gender
showmanship, 6
side show curiosity, 141
simplification, 8
skirts, 17
sleep, 135
Smith, Elinor, 200
Smith College, 51
smoking, 133, 134
Snook, Neta, xiii
social work, 67–68, 113, 142, 168, 203
society, 105
souvenirs, 140, 141, 145, 158
sports, 6, 136
spring cleaning hysteria, 105
St. Louis, 161
Stone, Lucy, 117. *See also* Lucy Stone League
Strandenaes, Brynjulf, 201
Stultz, Wilmer (Bill), xiv, 19, 22, 25
stunt flying, 1, 6, 22, 34, 42
subsidies, 76
success, ix, 129
Swedish, 176
swimming, 172

talent, 91
taxes, 84
telephone, 24

Texas, 162
Thaden, Louise, x, 157, 201
theater, 172
thrill, 5, 6, 26, 158
Tide and Time, 202
Toledo, 163
tomboy, 202
torchbearer, 169
Toronto, xiii, 81
tradition, 15, 99, 104, 152
train. *See* railroad
training, 13, 104
transatlantic solo flight (1932), 160, 179
Transcontinental Air Transport, xiv, 42
transportation, 45, 51–55, 72, 109, 180
trousers, 17
Trumble, Walter, 202
20 Hrs., 40 Min.: Our Flight in the Friendship, xi, xiv

urine, 28

Van Riper, A. Bowdoin, ix
Vega airplane. *See* Lockheed Vega
Vidal, Eugene, 75, 77, 112, 172, 202
Vidal, Gore, 2, 112, 203
Voluntary Aid Detachment, xiii, 81

wages, 71, 107
Wald, Lillian, 203

war, 81–86
wealth, 58
weather, 47
White, William Allen, 203
White House, 19, 144, 147–48
will, 164–65
Willebrandt, Mabel Walker, 172
Williams, Al, 204
Wilson, Woodrow, 20
women, 36, 43, 52, 60, 126, 160, 171, 183, 189, 190, 194, 197, 200; accidents, 157; in aviation, 6, 8, 10–17, 45, 97, 143, 171, 177, 193, 202; as drivers, 105; education, 90–92; in the home, 104, 105, 126; as pioneers, 154; rights, 77; sphere, 104; in sports, 136; in war, 81–86; work, 68–73, 100–101
Women's Air Derby, xiv, 25
work, 65–73, 101–2
Works Progress Administration, 76
World War I, xiii, 1, 81, 85
World War II, x
worry, 130
Wright brothers, 1
writing, 92

yacht, 6
youth, 3, 43, 45, 94, 108–9, 165